A. M. HUNTER

# The Gospel According to St Paul

SCM PRESS LTD

This book is a revised and in places much expanded version of *Interpreting Paul's Gospel* (SCM Press 1954).

© A. M. Hunter 1966

334  00593  0

First published 1966
by SCM Press Ltd
58 Bloomsbury Street, London WC1
Second impression 1978

Printed in Great Britain by
Fletcher & Son Ltd, Norwich

# CONTENTS

# PREFACE

MY HOPE is that this little book will provide the general reader, as well as the theological student, with a short, reliable and up-to-date sketch of St Paul's theology plus (in the last chapter) a suggestion that Paul still has something to say to us.

I have taken all the epistles commonly ascribed to Paul (including Ephesians) to be genuine, except the Pastorals.

The quotations are normally made from the RSV, but I have here and there availed myself of the felicities of the NEB.

A.M.H.

*King's College,*
*Aberdeen University*
February 1966

# 1

## THE BACKGROUND

ST PAUL was a Jew, living mostly in a Gentile or Greek environment, who had become a Christian. The background of his theology is therefore threefold: Jewish, Greek and Christian.

His debt to the Old Testament and Judaism is so plain on every page he wrote that one is left wondering how some German scholars (e.g. Pfleiderer and Reitzenstein) ever succeeded in persuading anyone that his thought was saturated with Greek ideas and religion. To be sure, he learned his Judaism in a Hellenistic *milieu*—unless van Unnik[1] is right, as he may well be, that Paul was 'brought up' in Jerusalem (Acts 22.3) where he went from Tarsus as a very small boy— but the burden of proof lies on all who would maintain that Hellenistic Judaism of the kind Paul knew differed greatly from its Palestinian counterpart.

'A Hebrew of the Hebrews' (Phil. 3.5), i.e. a Hebrew born and bred, is his own comment on his spiritual pedigree. Theologically speaking, this meant that he was reared in the *Credo* of the devout Jew of his time, viz. belief in one God righteous and holy, in the election of Israel to be his special People, in the Law (or *Torah*) as the unique revelation of God's nature and will for man, and in the hope of the Messiah.

His letters show that, even when he became a Christian, these things remained basic to his thought. Even if his letters and Acts had not told us that he belonged to the sect of the

[1] *Tarsus or Jerusalem*—City of Paul's Youth (London, 1963).

Pharisees and had received a rabbinical education, we should infer this from his theology. Nor let us despise these ultra-Jewish origins. 'If God was not moving in the rabbinic thought of Christ's day,' says Forsyth, 'what reason have we to say that he moves in the thought of today?'

In any case, the proof of his Jewishness is everywhere. Radically Jewish is his attitude to history. (Whereas the Greek saw the time-process as eternal recurrence, leading nowhere, Paul, like the prophets, saw it as the meaningful record of God's interventions in history, from creation to consummation.) Jewish too is his antithesis between 'spirit' and 'flesh', since it reflects the Jewish doctrine of the two inclinations. His favourite phrase 'in Christ' we can understand only in terms of the Jewish conception of 'corporate personality'. Would any but 'a Hebrew of the Hebrews' have called Jesus 'the last Adam'? When Paul discusses the Christian hope, it is the (Hebrew) resurrection of the body, not the (Greek) immortality of the soul which concerns him. And when he dwells on the last end of God's purpose in history, he says, very characteristically, 'And so all Israel will be saved' (Rom. 11.26).

'One of the great figures of Greek literature' is how a great 'Grecian' of our time—Gilbert Murray—has described Paul. What did this 'Hebrew of the Hebrews' owe to Hellenism? (N.B. We must not imagine that Jews and Greeks lived wholly apart. In fact, Jewish and Gentile thought were subject to what the botanists call 'cross-fertilization'.)

Paul read his scriptures normally in a Greek translation —the Septuagint, which was the Bible of the Apostolic Church. He wrote his letters in the 'Common Greek' which influence of all this upon him. Twice he quotes the Greek was the international language of the time. He spent most of his thirty years as a Christian in lands where Greek culture and civilization met him at every turn. We may not deny the poets ('We are also his offspring', Acts 17.28, Aratus; 'Bad company ruins good morals', I Cor. 15.33, Menander). He borrows illustrations from the Greek games—running, boxing, wrestling, the arena—and the Graeco-Roman processes of law, e.g. 'adoption'. Here and there he employs words from Greek popular moral philosophy like 'virtue' and 'conscience' or a Stoic doctrine like that of 'the law written on the heart'—the innate knowledge of the eternal principles of right and wrong (Rom. 2.14f.). Sometimes words used by the devotees of the Greek Mystery Religions, like 'mystery' and 'initiate', fall from his pen. But the idea that he was a zealous student of Greek letters or was deeply influenced by Stoic philosophy is not to be taken seriously; and the theory, fashionable fifty years ago in Germany, that his thinking about the sacraments was radically infected by the Mysteries has completely lost caste in the world of scholarship.

In short, if we may not deny Paul's debt to Hellenism, we must not overrate it. Books like Davies's *Paul and Rabbinic Judaism* show how Jewish his thought was at the grass roots. Oman once observed truly, 'The stronger a man's natural quality, the more likely it is to remain racy of his native soil.' Though the surface of Paul's thought may owe much to Hellenism, its sub-soil remained Jewish.

Now consider Paul's Christian debt. What did he owe to those who were 'in Christ' before him, like Ananias, Andronicus and Junias (Rom. 16.7), not to mention the members of the Mother Church in Jerusalem?

First, the Gospel which he preached, as he tells us in I Cor. 15.3ff., where, after quoting its chief *credenda*, he comments, 'What matter I or they [Peter, James, John and the rest]? This is what we all proclaim.' But this is only one among many things. Recent studies in 'the Twilight Period' of the Church (say AD 30-50) have made it very clear how many stones in the great edifice of what we once called

'Paulinism' were hewn into rough shape before the 'master-builder' took them over. Here we will content ourselves with listing seven: (1) the apostolic *kerygma* (already mentioned); (2) the confession of Jesus as Messiah, Lord and Son of God; (3) the doctrine of the Holy Spirit as the divine dynamic of the new life; (4) the conception of the Church as the New Israel; (5) the sacraments of Baptism and the Lord's Supper; (6) 'the Words of the Lord' which Paul quotes or echoes in his letters; and (7) the hope of the *Parousia*—or Christ's coming in glory.

Thus we err if we think of Paul as some kind of spiritual Columbus 'voyaging through strange seas of thought alone'. Original he was, and his own deep religious experience counted for much; but the thing about which he writes with such creative power was the common Christian faith which stemmed from those who were 'in Christ' before him.

Our prolegomena to Paul have still to mention what some have called 'the key to his theology'—his conversion.[1]

It has been well said that Paul's theology bears not so much the grammarian's as the sinner's touch and that what is needed for understanding it is not Higher Criticism but 'despair'. It is the theology of a converted man—a twice-born man—of one who could say, 'By the grace of God I am what I am.'

No doubt it took time for all the implications of the Damascus Road experience to become plain to him; but we may fairly say that it brought with it three decisive consequences.

To begin with, it meant that Jesus was incontrovertibly alive—alive by the power of God. What Paul saw convinced

[1] Jeremias traces no less than ten things to the Damascus Road experience, viz. our three items plus (4) predestination, (5) sense of sin, (6) opposition to legalism, (7) his Christian hope, (8) his missionary obligation, (9) his apostolic authority and (10) his doctrine of the Church. See *The Expository Times*, Oct. 1964, 27-30.

him (*a*) that he was in touch with a living and exalted Person; and (*b*) that this Person was none other than the crucified Jesus of Nazareth. Now Paul could go to the Christian community and confess, 'This Jesus of yours *is* the Messiah.'

Second: the Cross itself, which for Paul the Pharisee had been the place of God's curse (Deut. 21.23), became for him the place of revelation—the revelation of God's atoning love. Consider Gal. 3.13 (as translated for us by Jeremias);[1] 'God made him (Christ) a cursed one for us.' Where did this shocking expression come from if not from his pre-conversion days when 'Jesus is accursed' (Cf. I Cor. 12.3) was his watchword? After the risen Christ had appeared to him, he still went on saying it; only now he added the two pregnant words 'for us'.

Third: Paul knew now that 'salvation is of the Lord', that it begins on the divine side with an act of pure grace which man has done nothing to deserve. Small wonder that thereafter the grace (*charis*) of God, i.e. the favour of God to undeserving men—became almost a single-word expression for the Gospel he preached.[2]

[1] J. Jeremias, *The Central Message of the New Testament* (London, 1965), 35f.

[2] *Charis* occurs 88 times in his letters. Originally *charis* meant 'that which gives pleasure': charm, attractiveness. When the old Greeks used it centuries before Christ, they linked the word with loveliness, especially of form. Even in Hellenistic Judaism it is rarely used in a religious sense: only thrice in the LXX does it translate the Hebrew word for God's mercy—*hesed*. Then came the Gospel—and Paul—baptizing the word with new meaning, and henceforth 'grace' became twin-sister not to loveliness but love—the love of God for undeserving men. So what began as a *shining* word ended up as a *loving* one, and grace in the New Testament (as Denney classically defined it) 'is the love of God, spontaneous, beautiful, unearned at work in Jesus Christ for the salvation of sinful men'. (*Thessalonians*, 15.)

# 2

## SALVATION AS A PAST EVENT

WE ARE ready now to study St Paul's Christianity. But here the question arises: Is there any key word or concept which will lead us, as with an Ariadne's thread, to the heart of it, and enable us to see it it as a whole?

Traditional Protestantism, following Luther with his watchword *sola fide*, has found the heart of Paul's Gospel in the doctrine of 'justification by faith'. A true instinct guided them in this, since it fell to Paul—in conflict with Judaizers —to interpret the Fact of Christ in terms of righteousness and to show that true religion is a matter of a right relationship with God, and not primarily a matter of ethics and moral striving. But it is wrong to say that this doctrine epitomizes Paul's Gospel. For justification by faith is only the fragment of a larger whole—the first step on the Christian road, not the whole journey.

More recently scholars like Deissmann have summed up Paul's Gospel as 'communion with Christ'. Once again, this is but an element, though a very important one, in Paul's Christianity. What we need is a more comprehensive word to express the richness and range of Christianity according to St Paul; and the best word at our disposal is 'salvation' (*sōtēria*).

The fundamental question for religion is the Philippian gaoler's: 'What must I do to be saved?' Paul's religion starts from this question, and he finds the answer in what he calls 'the gospel of your salvation' (Eph. 1.13). When he preached in Pisidian Antioch or wrote to the Christians in Rome, this was the word he used (Acts 13.26; Rom. 1.16).

The word 'salvation' signified well-being in all its forms, from soundness of body to the highest ideal of spiritual health. And salvation was, in a sense, what all serious-minded men in Paul's day, Gentiles no less than Jews, were seeking. For the Jew salvation would mean primarily deliverance from the sin which separates from a holy God. For the Gentile, it would mean deliverance from all 'the slings and arrows of outrageous fortune', from Fate, fear of death and all the nameless insecurity on which we mortals hold the lease of life. But, however they construed the word, *sōtēria* was what both sought; and in the Gospel Paul claimed he had the answer to their longings ('the power of God unto salvation'), an answer in terms of the grace of God revealed in the Cross of Jesus Christ. Nor was the Gospel, in Paul's view, a mere remedial system—something negative—security from the long-term consequences of sin or from the haunting fear of annihilation. It included not only what a man must be saved *from* but also what he must be saved *to* —reconciliation and righteousness and life.

When Paul thought about Christian salvation, he saw it as a word with three tenses. It meant a past event, a present experience, and a future hope. 'We were saved,' he says in one place (Rom. 8.24). 'We are being saved,' he says in another (I Cor. 15.2). And 'we shall be saved,' he says in a third (Rom. 5.9). Indeed, Rom. 5.1 takes in all three tenses: 'Therefore being justified by faith, we have peace with God through our Lord Jesus Christ, through whom also we have obtained access into this grace in which we stand, and rejoice in hope of the glory of God.'

As Paul thinks of salvation, he looks back to the time when, by faith, the believer received God's forgiveness in Christ; he dwells on his present blessedness ('this grace wherein we stand'), and he looks forward to the time when, with sin and death no more, he will see God's splendour 'face to face'.

Our exposition of Paul's theology will be simply an expansion of this pregnant verse in Romans.

### Salvation as a Past Event

Salvation as a past event rests on the 'finished work of Christ'—what he did for men on the Cross—and looks back to the time when the sinner, by the decision of faith, made that deliverance his own.

The thing from which we need saving is sin, indwelling sin, that radical and corporate wrongness which separates us from God and in which every son of Adam shares.

It is in Romans that Paul's fullest teaching about it is to be found. There he shows two things—the universality of sin and the historical process by which it has come about, besides giving us a graphic picture in Rom. 7 of the power of sin in the flesh. (1) In Rom. 1.18-3.20, discussing the human wickedness which 'stifles' God's truth and provokes his displeasure, he shows how first Gentiles and then Jews come short of the glory of God, clinching his argument that all are sinners by appeal to scripture. (2) Then in Rom. 5.12-19 he discusses the Fall and its consequences. Adam's disobedience, he says, affected not himself only but all men. In Adam, the ancestor of the race, sin got a footing in the flesh; and since all mankind is one flesh with Adam, sin keeps its hold on the flesh from generation to generation. This is a doctrine of universal, but not total, depravity. All men, Paul would say, are tainted by it. Born into this tainted society, man is from his earliest days subject to the power of sin.

For Paul, then, sin is not a *defect* (as for the Greeks) but a *defection*; neither is it (as for the moralist) a mere incident, without antecedents or consequences, a series of wrong choices. It is a universal state, nay, rather, a positive and destructive principle or power, endemic in man and enslaving him ('sold under sin' we become its slaves, Rom. 6.17, 7.14) so that, to get Paul's full meaning, we have almost to spell it with a capital S.

The effect of sin is to bring man under God's wrath (Rom. 1.18, 4.15) which is not his 'rage' or bad temper, but his holy love reacting against evil—the adverse wind of his will blowing against the sinner now as well as at Judgment Day.

Such sin (Paul says), unless effectively dealt with, must finally prove fatal—'the wage sin pays is death' (Rom. 6.23). The cure for it is 'the redemption which is in Christ Jesus' (Rom. 3.24).

The tool which sin uses is the *flesh* (*sarx*),[1] a word found some 90 times in Paul's letters and reflecting the meaning of *basar* in OT passages like Isa. 31.3 and Jer. 17.5.[2] Paul uses it in two broad ways—with or without a moral connotation.

Basically, flesh is the *material* side of man's nature and is morally neutral. It can describe man's physical make-up and his natural ties, but it can also express the idea of man in the solidarity of his worldly existence, as of man in his weakness and mortality over-against God.

But, second, every reader of Paul will recall places (e.g. Rom. 7 and 8 and Gal. 5) where flesh acquires an *ethical* meaning and is definitely associated with sin. Paul does not mean that the flesh is inherently and intrinsically evil, but he does regard it as corrupted. The corrupter is sin. Sin (he

[1] This is not the same as the body (*sōma*) which in Paul means the principle of individuality, subsisting through all changes of substance.
[2] As also the influence of the rabbinical doctrine of the evil inclination.

says), using our weak flesh as 'a base of operations' (*aphormē*, Rom. 7.11; Gal. 5.13), has corrupted it. Or, to put it another way, flesh has become the unwilling accomplice of sin, which is the real criminal. So, flesh, as the material which gives sin its chance, comes to mean 'our lower nature' —man as fallen and apostate from God.

To 'live after the flesh' (*kata sarka*) is not so much to live sensually (though that comes into it) as to live Godlessly, in sinful self-reliance. It means to turn away from the Creator and find one's security in the creation which is transient and perishable. The opposite to this is 'living by the Spirit'; and as 'living after the flesh' produces ruin and death, so living by the Spirit brings life and peace (Rom. 8.5f.). In short (as Barth says) the flesh in Paul 'stands for the complete inadequacy of the creature before his Creator' for which the sole remedy is 'the Spirit of life in Christ Jesus' (Rom. 8.2).

The last member in the terrible triumvirate from which man needs to be delivered is the Law, primarily the Law of Moses, but that Law as an expression of the universal law of God.

St Paul speaks of 'the curse of the law' (Gal. 3.13). Yet elsewhere he can call it 'holy' and say it was meant to 'give life' (Rom. 7.10, 12). How can the law be described in one place as the holy demand of God and in another as a slavery driving a man to despair? The explanation is that it is not the law as such (which, so far as it contains the moral demands of God, remains valid) but 'legalism' which is the curse. Legalism is the attempt to 'live'—to find salvation— under the law, by obeying its statutes and so earning credit in the ledgers of heaven. It is believing you can be and do good in your own strength. The 'legal' man is the religiously 'self-made man'. But, as Paul found—and countless others have found since—not that way lies salvation. No man can earn God's favour by 'works of law'. Let mortal man present himself before the Most High clad in works of law (as the Pharisee tried to do in Christ's parable) and the verdict must always be 'Unrighteous'.

So Paul came to a clear conclusion. The law is powerless to save—powerless, as he put it, because it 'is weak through the flesh' (Rom. 8.3). He came to another—one which we too can verify for ourselves: the law produces a sense of sin, and even provokes to sinning (Rom. 3.20, 7.7; I Cor. 15.56)—as the command 'Thou shalt not steal' drove the youthful Augustine to raid a neighbour's orchard. So, thirdly, Paul came to see the purpose of the law as preparatory. It is (he argues) a temporary expedient in God's plan (Rom. 5.20; Gal. 3.17), or, more positively, a *paidagōgos*—a guardian and tutor to discipline us until the coming of God's promised salvation in Christ (Gal. 3.24). For, with Christ's coming, the day of the law as a way of salvation is over (Rom. 10.4). In Christ there becomes possible a new relationship—that of sonship to God—one in which God's law is written on the heart, in which love constrains to its doing, and in which the Spirit is the power by which it is done. 'Now discharged from the law,' Paul writes (Rom. 7.6, NEB), 'we serve God in a new way, the way of the spirit, in contrast to the old way, the way of a written code.'

So Paul diagnosed our human predicament in terms of sin, the flesh and the law. When he spoke of God's remedy for it, the Gospel, he employed three picture-phrases: redemption, justification, and reconciliation. The first which sees our plight as servitude comes from the slave-market. The second which sees it as condemnation comes from the law-court. The third which sees it as alienation comes from personal relations.

First, salvation is Redemption (Greek: *apolutrosis*: 'deliverance', 'emancipation') from servitude, servitude to indwelling sin, servitude to the yoke of the law, servitude to all the unseen spiritual powers which were believed to bedevil human existence.[1]

'In Christ', he said, 'we have redemption' (Rom. 3.24; Eph. 1.7; Col. 1.14). 'Christ redeemed us from the curse of the law' (Gal. 3.13). 'You have been set free from sin' (Rom. 6.22). This metaphor of redeeming (however strange to us today who can think only of the pawnshop) was well calculated to come home to people familiar with slavery and the custom of 'sacral manumission', i.e. the fictitious purchase of a slave by deity whereby he regained his freedom. (The owner would accompany his slave to a temple and sell him to the god, e.g. Serapis. In return he received from the temple treasury the purchase-money—*lutron*—previously paid in by the slave out of his own earnings. Then, when the necessary documents had been signed, the slave became the property of the god but, in the eyes of all the world and his master in particular, a free man.) But the word 'redemption' would also inevitably recall the first great deliverance of God's people from Egyptian bondage. Moreover, when Paul told his converts, 'You were bought with a price' (I Cor. 6.20), he may well have been echoing his Lord's great 'ransom-saying' (Mark 10.45); cf. I Tim. 2.5f.

The means of redemption was of course the deed of the Cross, and the rescue for sinners accomplished there by One who was the Second Adam and Head of a new humanity. By faith in him, Paul said, men could now be free from all those evil powers to which they had once been in bondage.

If the first barrier to salvation was servitude to other powers than God, the second was condemnation on the ground of sin and transgression. God's remedy for this was *justification*.

The Greek verb for 'justify' is *dikaiō*. But what precisely

[1] See the Note at the end of this chapter.

does it mean? 'Make righteous'? No, say the philologists. 'Declare righteous'? This is the common Protestant view. 'Acquit'? The metaphor certainly was forensic in origin, and that meaning still survives in some of Paul's contexts, e.g. Rom. 8.32f. But the opinion is growing among scholars that, though originally forensic, the verb on Paul's lips has for the most part become soteriological and means 'forgive' or 'pardon'. Certainly it is so in Rom. 4.6-8. Perhaps then we may settle for the meaning 'set right' with the connotation of 'forgive'. 'Justification', says Jeremias, 'is forgiveness, nothing but forgiveness, for Christ's sake.'[1]

Justification is essentially getting into right relations with God. This, Paul says, no man can do for himself. Only God can do it. Justification is God's gracious way of forgiving men—of 'setting them right' with himself—for Christ's sake.

Let us consider for a moment Paul's key-phrase 'the righteousness of God'. In the Gospel, he says, 'the righteousness of God has been revealed through faith for faith' (Rom. 1.17). Here righteousness is not so much an attribute as an *activity* of God. It is, as the NEB translates, 'God's way of righting wrong'. When Paul as a Jew thought about the righteousness of God, he thought of the righteous God in action, God working out a righteous purpose, God putting things right for his people by rescuing them from their oppressors or delivering them from their sin—that consummation long devoutly desired by Old Testament prophet and psalmist (cf. Isa. 56.1 and Psalm 98.2 where 'righteousness' means God's saving and vindicating activity). Now, says Paul, in the events of the Gospel Story—in the Fact of Christ—God is to be openly seen doing what is needed for

[1] *The Central Message of the New Testament*, 57. According to T. W. Manson, *On Paul and John* (London, 1963), 57, justification is a *regal* rather than a *judicial* act, and means amnesty or free pardon; cf. John Wesley: 'The plain scriptural notion of justification is pardon, the forgiveness of sins.'

men's deliverance, and so making possible that new relationship with himself which men need in order to be saved.

The question 'What must a sinner do to get right with God?' then becomes, How is he to make this Divine righteousness his own? And the answer is: By faith in Christ whom God has made 'our righteousness'. When a sinful man commits himself in faith to Christ, who died for our sins, God of his grace sets him right with himself, justifies him. This means not only pardon for his sins but the gift of a new standing with God. This does not make the man at once sinless; but the justified man is potentially righteous; and he is called on to become all that he is in germ.

'God', Paul says, 'justifies the ungodly' (Rom. 4.5). There is paradox here, for something of the law-court still clings to the verb. 'God acquits guilty men' is how the NEB renders it. But through the forensic language we glimpse the amazing grace of God, and, at bottom, Paul is proclaiming the same truth as Jesus in his greatest parable. There, in the language not of the law-court but of the home, we see God, in a figure, 'justifying the ungodly'. The father's kiss, it has been said, is justification (as the ring and the robe are glorification). And justification is the first and decisive step on the road to salvation.

So we come to Paul's third and last term for salvation as a past event: 'reconciliation'.

The Greek noun is *katallagē*, the verb *katallassō* or (in Eph. and Col.) *apokatallassō*. The chief passages are Rom. 5.10-11; II Cor. 5.18-20; Eph. 2.16; and Col. 1.19ff. (where we have not only a cosmic Christ and a cosmic cross, but also the promise of a cosmic peace). And the basic idea is of restoration to fellowship with God.

This, we may well judge, is Paul's best way of putting it, because it lifts the whole issue from the level of the law-court to the plane of personal relations; because, too, the hunger for reconciliation with reality—from primitive man's attempts to keep on good terms with an unchancy unseen world to Augustine's confession that 'our hearts are restless till they rest in thee'—is something elemental and universal.

It is sin which creates the need for reconciliation. Sin destroys that fellowship with God for which man was made. It sets up an estranging barrier between the holy God and his creature man. It interrupts the family relationship. Paul's name for this state is 'alienation' (Eph. 4.18; Col. 1.21). Man's need is to recover the lost fellowship, to be restored to God's family circle, to get out of dis-grace into grace. But this he cannot do for himself. Only God can do it for him. And, says Paul, it is the heart of the Gospel that God has done it—in Christ and his Cross:

'In Christ God was reconciling the world to himself' (II Cor. 5.19).[1]

'For if while we were enemies we were reconciled to God by the death of his Son, much more, now that we are reconciled, shall we be saved by his life' (Rom. 5.10).

'For in him all the fulness of God (i.e. God in his fulness) was pleased to dwell, and through him to reconcile all things, whether on earth or in heaven, making peace by the blood of his cross' (Col.1.19f.).

To such doctrine Greek religion provides no parallel, nor does Judaism, for in Judaism God is reconciled to man, not man to God. In Paul, *per contra*, God is always the subject, man the object, in reconciliation. No doubt when men obey the summons 'Be reconciled to God' (II Cor. 5.20) and the estranging barrier falls away, a new situation—a change in relations—arises for God as well as for man; but this is quite another thing from saying that God is reconciled.

[1] The AV's 'God was in Christ, reconciling the world to himself' is almost certainly wrong. See Plummer, ICC, *ad loc.*

What is changed for man is not his legal status but his whole life. He becomes 'a new creature' (*Kainē ktisis*,[1] II Cor. 5.17). The old has gone; the new has come.

The means of reconciliation is 'the death of his Son', so that, as always in Paul, we are back at the Cross. To ask how the Cross effects reconciliation is to ask, What is Paul's doctrine of the Atonement?

This is too big a question to be answered in a paragraph or two; but let us try to take the main points.

The first one is that Paul did not invent the doctrine. That 'Christ died for our sins according to the scriptures' (I Cor. 15.3, with the reference almost certainly to Isaiah 53) was part of the tradition Paul received from his Christian predecessors; and for Paul, as for all the apostolic men, the Cross was 'the hiding place of God's power and the inspiration of all Christian praise'.

Yet so variously does he write about it that it is foolish to try to confine his doctrine in a single phrase. Now he sees the Cross as the supreme proof of the divine love: 'God shows his love for us in that while we were yet sinners Christ died for us' (Rom. 5.8. How axiomatic it is for Paul that God was in what Christ did on the Cross!). Now he sees it as the lifting by Christ of the curse that lay on us as breakers of the law (Gal. 3.13); now as a sacrifice for sin (Rom. 8.3); and now as a victory over the demonic powers (Col. 2.15).

But if we would penetrate more deeply into Paul's thought two cardinal passages demand more detailed study.

First, Rom. 3.24ff.:

'They are justified by his grace as a gift, through the redemption that is in Christ Jesus, whom God put forward

---

[1] *Kainē ktisis*—the Hebrew *beriyyah hedashah*, a common rabbinical phrase for a man brought to the true knowledge of God. See J. B. Lightfoot, *Galatians*, 224.

as an expiation by his blood, to be received by faith. This was to show God's righteousness, because in his divine forbearance he had passed over former sins; it was to prove in the present time that he himself is righteous and that he justifies him who has faith in Jesus.'

The crux here is the meaning of *hilastērion*. The AV's 'propitiation' will not do, for linguistic[1] as well as theological reasons. The choice lies between (*a*) the general 'expiation' (as in the RSV above) and (*b*) a reference to the OT 'mercy seat' (*kapporeth*, rendered by *hilastērion* in the LXX). If (*a*) be preferred, the Cross is the place where God expiates, i.e. annuls or neutralizes, that in man which unfits him for communion with God. But the usage of the Greek OT perhaps makes likelier a reference to the 'mercy seat' which was for the Jew the locus of God's mercy and forgiveness.[2] In that case Christ replaces the mercy seat in the Holy of Holies; and what was symbolized in the ritual of the Day of Atonement is actualized in him.

The Cross is such because of two things: (1) 'his blood', i.e. the self-sacrifice of Christ; and (2) the faith of believers.

Why did God thus 'put forward' Christ? To make his saving goodness clear and convincing. Before Calvary there had been no radical dealing with sin. God could only bear patiently with men, overlooking but not condoning their sin. But with the Cross comes the proof that God is not only himself righteous but also accepts sinners who put faith in Jesus.

Second, II Cor. 5.18ff. Here Paul first tells us (14) that Christ's was a representative death ('one has died for all; therefore all have died'); then after declaring that the atonement means the cancellation of men's sins (19), he comes to

[1] C. H. Dodd, *The Bible and the Greeks* (London, 1935), 82-95; *Romans* (London, 1932), 54f.
[2] T. W. Manson, *Journal of Theological Studies*, 46, 1945, 1-10.

his climactic statement: 'For our sake he made him to be sin who knew no sin, so that in him we might become the righteousness of God.' We are reminded of the verse in Galatians (3.13, discussed earlier) that 'God made Christ a cursed one for us'. Christ made sin for our sakes! One wonders if the OT scapegoat is somewhat in the background of his thought. Paul sees the Cross as an act of God's appointing in which the sinless One, for the sake of sinners, somehow experienced the horror of the divine reaction against sin, that for us there might be condemnation no more.

Passages like these reveal the holy love of God taking awful issue in the Cross with the sin of man. Christ, by God's will, dies the sinner's death and so removes sin. Is there a simpler way of saying all this than that Christ bore our sins and that his sufferings were what, for lack of a better word, we can only call 'penal'?[1]

One thing more. For Paul the Cross is never to be isolated from the Resurrection. 'If Christ be not raised, you are yet in your sins' (I Cor. 15.17) for Christ 'was delivered up for our trespasses and raised for our justification' (Rom. 4.25). We are saved by the living Crucified.

Redemption, justification, reconciliation—all through the Cross of Christ—such are the ways in which Paul describes God's saving work as a past event. But man has to make God's gift his own, and the word for taking what God gives is *faith*.

The word which, as noun or verb, occurs almost 200 times in Paul, can carry various shades of meaning according to the context: 'faithfulness', for example, as in Rom. 3.3;

[1] Some people instinctively boggle at the word 'penal'—rightly, if the suggestion is that God punished Christ; but wrongly, if they fail to realize that an innocent person can be involved in the penal sufferings of others, either through accident, or because he deliberately chooses in love to identify himself with sinners.

conviction of the unseen, as in II Cor. 5.7; and in Gal. 1.23 it is almost a synonym for Christianity. But the truly Pauline meaning of the word is trust—utter trust—as its Old Testament exemplar *par excellence* is 'the father of the faithful', Abraham, who when God spoke to him took God at his word and obeyed (see Rom. 4). Faith for Paul is taking God at his word in Christ, and it has a strong element of obedience—compare Rom. 1.5 'the obedience of faith', the obedience which consists in faith. Nor is the element of belief absent. As Abraham believed that God's promise to him was reliable, so Christian faith is the confident belief 'that Christ is not an illusion but the reality of God'.

Pauline faith we may further characterize as follows:

First, it is directed not to a proposition but to a person, sometimes God, sometimes Christ; but there is no difference of meaning, since for Paul it is axiomatic that God was in Christ.

Second, as the principle of salvation, it is opposed to 'works', i.e. every scheme of salvation by human effort, every attempt by meritorious acts to lay up 'credit' in heaven.

Third, faith is not only an act (as in Rom. 10.9) but an attitude of life: 'The life I now live in the flesh,' Paul says, 'I live by faith in the Son of God who loved me and gave himself for me' (Gal. 2.20). For the act of faith initiates a faith-union between the sinner and his Saviour (Luther likened it to a wedding ring), so that he enters into the virtue of all that Christ has done for him and lives henceforth in vital communion with his living Lord.

Fourth: the faith that commits us to Christ in the same act commits us to his community, the Church.

Finally faith, unless it is a sham (I Cor. 13.2), operates through love (Gal. 5.6) and issues in 'good works'. Or, put more simply, the good live by faith and work by love. For though Paul rejected 'works' as a *condition* of salvation, no one more firmly demanded them as a *consequence* of it.

Of the reality of this faith baptism is the *seal*. (See Rom. 4.11 and the passages where Paul speaks of being 'sealed': II Cor. 1.22; Eph. 1.13, 4.30. In baptism the convert is stamped as the property of the Lord.)

For Paul, as for his Christian predecessors, baptism was the rite of initiation into the Church. Its mode was immersion. Administered to adults upon profession of faith ('Jesus is Lord'; cf. Rom 10.9), it was 'in the name of the Lord Jesus Christ' (I Cor. 6.11) and was normally associated with the reception of the Spirit (I Cor. 12.13).

To set forth the meaning of the sacrament, Paul uses various illustrations. In baptism, he says, you were 'washed' (I Cor. 6.11); and the point is cleansing from the impurity of their old life. Again, in baptism, you 'put on Christ' (like a garment: Gal. 3.17. The convert robed afresh after immersion); and his point is their union with the living Lord. Again, in baptism, you were 'baptized into one body' (I Cor. 12.13); and the point is incorporation into the mystical Body of Christ, the Church. Baptismal, too, is probably the context in which he tells his converts, 'You are adopted sons of God who cry Abba Father' (Rom. 8.15; Gal. 4.6); and the point is inclusion in God's family.

In two passages (Rom. 6.3ff. and Col. 2.12) Paul describes baptism as the believer's dying with Christ to sin and rising with him into newness of life. To understand the 'realism' of his language here, we must remember that behind Christian baptism stands the great Baptism of Christ himself (cf. Mark 10.38 and Luke 12.50), unique and all-inclusive, undertaken by Christ himself for the sins of the whole world.[1] It is into the virtue of that once-for-all Baptism that

[1] Cf. Oscar Cullmann, *Baptism in the New Testament* (London, 1950), 23. 'According to the New Testament, all men have in prin-

a man enters when he professes his faith in his Lord and is 'baptized into Christ'.

We must also remember that the physical movements of the sacrament—descent into the water, immersion and emersion—made a vivid symbol of the thing signified. Only a symbol? No, something more. If Paul's stress on the primacy of faith precludes the idea that the sacrament operated automatically, what we know of Old Testament 'prophetic symbolism' suggests we have here a corporate application of it.[1] In other words, the act of baptism was an earnest of what would be—it set forward, helped to realize, what it symbolized—death to the old life and resurrection to the new. But it was no magic, and the baptized person was henceforward under obligation to become what in principle he already was—a new man in Christ. Hence what have been called Paul's 'imperatives of grace': 'Put yourselves at the disposal of God, as dead men raised to life; yield your bodies to him as implements for doing right; for sin shall no longer be your master, because you are no longer under law, but under the grace of God' (Rom. 6.13f., NEB).

### NOTE ON THE PRINCIPALITIES AND POWERS

Human life in the first century AD was deeply shadowed by fear of the sinister unseen. Pitted against men, it was believed, was a hierarchy of invisible cosmic forces and tyrants. These were not simply the evil spirits afflicting men of which

---

ciple received baptism long ago, namely, on Golgotha, at Good Friday and Easter.'

[1] Cf. H. Wheeler Robinson, *The Christian Experience of the Holy Spirit* (London, 1928), 192ff.; G. B. Caird, *The Apostolic Age* (London, 1955), 48f.

we read in the Gospels. Ranged against men were what Paul variously calls 'principalities and powers', 'the rulers of this world', 'the elemental spirits of the universe', and 'the spiritual hosts of wickedness in the heavenly places', of which Satan was but the titular chief. Standing behind human authorities and institutions—Paul, for example, throws on these evil powers the responsibility for the crucifixion (I Cor. 2.8)—these 'discarnate Intelligences' (to borrow Thomas Hardy's phrase) exercised a malign influence on human affairs and held men in thrall.

(For a modern parallel we may go to the mission-field and observe the same phenomenon among peoples at the same level of civilization. They too live in a like bondage of fear to a sinister unseen world, and, as Schweitzer has said, for them 'Christianity is the light which shines in the darkness of their fear, for it assures man that he is not in the power of Nature-spirits or ancestral ghosts but in all that happens the will of God maintains its sovereignty'.)

St Paul of course speaks of these angelic powers in the language of his day—mythological language we should call it; but he is describing spiritual realities that belong to the experience of himself and his fellow-Christians, i.e. the language has a rational content. In his view these evil powers have, in principle, been defeated by Christ's victory in the Cross (Col. 2.15), but they are still operative, and their end will only come when 'Christ delivers the kingdom to God the Father after destroying every rule and every authority and power' (I Cor. 15.24).

In our day the outbreakings of irrational evil on a vast scale in human affairs have aroused men's interest afresh in what Paul has to say about demonic forces at work in the world—as witness the writings of C. S. Lewis and Paul Tillich. Not only has this led to fresh study of the origins of this belief—between the Exile and the Advent—in Israel's history (Israel's primitive belief in other gods existing in some kind of relation to Yahweh, astral religion from Babylonia, etc.); but it has led our theologians to apply Paul's teaching, in non-mythological terms, to the 'demonic' elements and authorities in modern life—secular false gods, neo-pagan dogmas which hold sway over men's imaginations and embody themselves in destructive institutions, and even (in C. S. Lewis) 'the demon capacities of an omnicompetent science'.

For the biblical side of all this the reader should consult G. B. Caird's *Principalities and Powers*,[1] and for the theological, the writings of Paul Tillich who apparently thought it possible that these evil powers were personal agents.

[1] Oxford, 1956.

# 3

## SALVATION AS A PRESENT EXPERIENCE

IF a man had been saved when by faith he responded to God's grace in Christ, it was equally true that he was now being saved. Salvation was a present and progressive experience.

Our forefathers would have called this the transition from justification to sanctification. Justification is, in Bunyan's metaphor, the wicket-gate admitting to the path towards the Celestial City. Sanctification is the path itself. It is the new Spirit-led life of moral progress, peace and joy—at once, as the Germans say, *Gabe und Aufgabe*—gift and task. 'Work out your own salvation,' Paul says, and in the next breath, 'for God is at work in you' (Phil. 2.13).

Salvation in this aspect Paul describes variously. Believers, he says, are in a new realm—'the kingdom of his dear Son' (Col. 1.13). They stand on a new platform, that of grace, 'this grace wherein we stand' (Rom. 5.2). They are in a new relationship with God, that of adopted sons, admitted to God's family (Gal. 4.5; Rom. 8.15). (Note: Paul uses the metaphor of adoption to mark the fact that we are sons of God by grace, whereas Christ is a Son by nature. Note also that in the child-father relation Jesus too saw the best picture of that fellowship with God, which is man's true destiny. Note finally that both Jesus and Paul teach that we *become* sons of God.)

Paul's most positive word for present salvation is Life, the life that is life indeed, because lived in the favour and fellowship of God. (Cf. John's doctrine of eternal life as something that begins here and now. John might have written Rom. 6.23, 'The free gift of God is eternal life in Christ Jesus our Lord.') 'He who through faith is righteous shall live' (Rom. 1.17). Justified sinners 'walk in newness of life' (Rom. 6.4). 'Christ died for us,' he says, 'that, whether we wake or sleep, we should live together with him' (I Thess. 5.10). Ideally—though Paul knows well how far we come short of our high calling—the marks of this new life are 'death to sin' and 'peace with God'—sinlessness and serenity —and it can be described as Life 'in Christ', or Life 'in the Spirit'.

I

Every reader of Paul's letters has noted the frequency of the phrase 'in Christ' or 'in the Lord'. If we count in by-forms like 'in him', the phrase occurs some 200 times. What does it mean?

Sometimes it appears to be no more than a substitute for the word 'Christian'. Thus Paul calls Onesimus 'a beloved brother . . . both in the flesh and in the Lord', which probably means no more than 'as man and as Christian' (Philemon 16).

But the phrase carries deeper suggestions than this. Doubtless it grew out of what Paul calls baptism 'into Christ' (Gal. 3.27). When a man was baptized 'into Christ', he passed into his possession, became 'in him'. Whatever else it means, 'in Christ' must mean 'in communion with Christ'. This experience was basic to Paul's Christianity, as it still is to any Christianity worthy of the name. The phrase will then describe 'the most intimate fellowship imaginable of the Christian with the living spiritual Christ' (Deissmann).[1]

[1] *St Paul*, 28.

B

Yet this is but half the truth. In many passages the phrase so clearly carries a corporate meaning that we have to translate 'in the fellowship of Christ'. The clue is to be sought in the Hebrew conception of corporate personality—a conception which enabled him to think of the community in terms of its representative head. Now we know that Paul thought of Christ in this corporate way—witness I Cor. 12.12: 'For just as the body is one and has many members,' Paul says, 'and all the members of the body, though many, are one body, so it is with Christ.' 'Paul calls Christ the Church,' comments John Calvin, and he is right.

We must say then that the phrase means not only 'in communion with Christ' but also 'in the community of Christ'. It describes a shared life, a *koinōnia*. It involves membership of the Church which is Christ's Body. So Floyd Filson[1] can write:

'To be "in Christ", while it is a great personal privilege and experience, is a privilege which inevitably puts a man into Church and binds him to his fellow-believers in the one body of Christ.'

Being 'in Christ' is therefore a social experience. What Paul has in mind is changed men and women living in a changed society, with Christ the author of the change in the individual, and Christ the living centre of the new environment in which they live.

The phrase 'in Christ' has made men talk about Paul's 'Christ mysticism'. But the kind of experience involved in it is not the sort one normally associates with mysticism—something solitary, mysterious, remote from everyday life, otherworldly. Look at some of the things that happen *en Christo*. 'In Christ' or 'in the Lord' Christians not only 'trust' (Phil. 2.24) and 'hope' (Phil. 2.19) and 'rejoice' (Phil. 3.1); they also 'tell the truth' (Rom. 9.1), 'work' and 'labour'

[1] *The New Testament against its Environment* (London, 1950), 77.

(Rom. 16.12; I Cor. 15.58), 'stand firm' (Phil. 4.1) and 'agree' (Phil. 4.2), 'welcome' travelling missionaries (Rom. 16.2), 'send greetings' (I Cor. 16.19) and 'get married' (I Cor. 7.39).

New life—shared life at all levels, high and humble—new life in a new community whose Head is the living Christ present through the Holy Spirit, this is what Paul means by being 'in Christ'.

*Note*. Deissmann probably erred in taking the phrase to be Paul's own coinage. (1) The idea is implicit in the Synoptic sayings which stress the solidarity of the Messiah with his people, e.g. Mark 8.38 (reading 'me and mine', with the NEB); Matt. 18.20; and above all Matt. 25.40-45.[1] (2) The phrase, or its equivalent, occurs in Acts and I Peter as well as in the 'Abide in me' of John 15.

II

But to be 'in Christ' was equally to be 'in the Spirit'. Note how often the phrase 'in the Spirit' is found with the same verbs and nouns as the phrase 'in Christ'. 'Sanctified in the Holy Spirit' (Rom. 15.16) is paralleled by 'sanctified in Christ Jesus' (I Cor. 1.2), as 'joy in the Holy Spirit' (Rom. 14.17) by 'rejoice in the Lord' (Phil. 3.1), and so on. Yet in spite of the statement 'the Lord is the Spirit' (II Cor. 3.17; cf. NEB 'Now the Lord of whom this passage speaks is the Spirit'),[2] Paul does not identify Christ with the Spirit. The truth is rather that it is through the Spirit that Christ comes

---

[1] Cf. Matt. 25.40, 'As you did it to one of the least of these my brethren, you did it to me,' with I Cor. 8.12, 'In thus sinning against your brothers . . . you sin against Christ.'

[2] The best explanation, known to me, of II Cor. 3.17 is in Denney's *Second Corinthians*, 133f.

to Christians. Theologically, Christ and the Spirit are distinguishable (as in the Apostolic benediction of II Cor. 13.14); experientially, they are one. For Paul the Holy Spirit is the *divine energy or dynamic* of the new life (see I Thess. 1.5; Rom. 15.13, 'the power of the Holy Spirit'): it is God's gracious power operating on and in man, yet never apart from Christ. This is why he can speak indifferently, as he does in Romans 8, of 'the Spirit of God', 'the Spirit of Christ', and 'Christ in you', meaning the self-same spiritual power. And always the Spirit stands for what we call the supernatural: not only God as a presence in man but God as a power transcending human experience.

Paul, of course, did not originate belief in the Holy Spirit. The Pentecostal Event (Acts 2) had made the Christian community signally aware of a strange new 'uprush of life' in their midst which they identified with the Spirit of God prophetically promised for the Messianic Age (Joel 2). But whereas the first Christians tended to regard it as the source of ecstatic religious 'experiences' like 'tongues' (*glōssolalia*) and what we would call 'revival phenomena', Paul saw it as the source of all religious experience, and of gifts which, if less spectacular, were far more serviceable. Thus I Cor. 14 shows that, if he had been compelled to arrange the gifts of the Spirit in order of merit, love (*agapē*) would have stood first and 'tongues' last.

It would be wrong to say that Paul was the first to *moralize* the Christian conception of the Spirit's working—that is, to regard it as the source and dynamic of what we would call 'the good life'—but by 'playing down' the unhealthy stress on ecstasy and 'tongues' in Corinth, he undoubtedly brought order into confusion and put first things first. Moreover, by his conception of the Spirit as 'leading', 'witnessing' and 'pleading'—see Romans 8—he helped to *personalize* men's thinking about it. Finally, by associating the Spirit with the living Christ, he helped to *christianize* (perhaps better 'christify') men's ideas of the Spirit. For the fruits of the Spirit—love, joy, peace, patience, kindness, goodness, fidelity, gentleness and self-control—are (as Schleiermacher said) essentially the virtues of Christ.

How wonderfully wide and rich is Paul's whole doctrine of the Spirit! Sharply opposed to 'the flesh' and the law, the Spirit creates power where there was weakness, freedom where there was servitude, and life where there was death.

It is the Spirit which pours the love of God into our hearts (Rom. 5.5), enables us to fulfil the law's requirements (Rom. 8.4), prompts us to cry 'Abba, Father' (Rom. 8.15f.), assists our faltering prayers (Rom. 8.26), produces the Christian virtues (Gal. 5.22), and is the pledge (*arrabōn*)[1] and first instalment of perfected salvation and immortal life (II Cor. 1.22, 5.5; Eph. 1.14). Finally it is the Spirit which, as Paul explains in I Cor. 2, enables the apostles to 'have the mind (*nous*) of Christ'—that is, to have not so much the temper as the *theology* of Christ, to divine Christ's saving intention, to have unique insight into the meaning of what God purposed and did in Christ.[2]

To sum up. The Spirit is God in Christ at work in men, helping, inspiring, illuminating, quickening, sanctifying. The Christian life is a life lived by its beneficent and blessed power. And, as the phrase 'the fellowship of the Spirit' (II Cor. 13.14; Phil. 2.1) reminds us, the Spirit 'knows nothing of solitary Christianity' but binds men together in the bonds of Christian 'togetherness'.

The Spirit is as central to Paul's Christianity as electricity to our modern civilization. The man who would know how

---

[1] *Arrabōn*, a commercial term, means a down payment by which the purchaser binds himself to complete the full payment agreed on.
[2] See P. T. Forsyth, *The Person and Place of Jesus Christ* (London, 1946), chap. 8.

central it is should ponder well Gal. 5, II Cor. 3, and, above all, Rom. 8, not forgetting I Cor. 12-14 which treats of the Spirit's 'charisms' or 'grace-gifts'. There the whole Christian life is guided, prompted and secured by the strong spirit of God.

III

If the Holy Spirit is the dynamic of the new life, the sphere in which it is lived is the Church.

When did the Church begin? Some have said: on the Day of Pentecost, with the advent of the Spirit. But would it not be truer to call that event the Church's 'coming of age'? The Church of Christ really began when Jesus called twelve men to be the symbolic nucleus of the new Israel he was founding, as, at the Last Supper, 'the Twelve sat as representatives of the *Ecclēsia* at large'. And for Paul, writing twenty or thirty years later, the Church is basically a pure communion of persons bound to the living Christ and to one another through the Holy Spirit. In his letters the apostle has various names for it: now it is 'the temple of God' (I Cor. 3.16); now it is 'the household of faith' (Gal. 6.10); and now it is 'the bride of Christ' (II Cor. 11.2; Eph. 5.25ff.: a nuptial symbol from the OT). But he thinks of the Church in two chief ways.

To begin with, it is *the true People of God*. Israel after the flesh, old Israel, claiming to be God's true People, have forfeited their claim by rejecting the Messiah, and the Christians have served themselves heirs to it. To be sure, once only (Gal. 6.16) does Paul call the Church 'the Israel of God'. But he is thinking of the Church as the true People of God when he addresses his readers as 'the saints' (*hoi hagioi*, which the NEB renders 'God's People'), or calls Christians 'the seed of Abraham' (Gal. 3.29), or likens the Church to an

Olive Tree with native and wild shoots (i.e. Jews and Gentiles, now united in Christ: Rom. 11.17-24). These phrases, which have Old Testament roots, underline the continuity of the Church of Christ with the ancient people of God. But the Church is no less a new creation, reconstituted by the blood of the New Covenant and inaugurated by the Resurrection and the gift of the Spirit. For this new creation the old ceremonial laws no longer apply, and with Christ's abolition of 'the middle wall of partition' (Eph. 2.14) between Jew and Gentile, nationality has ceased to count: open to all who have faith, the potential bounds of the new People of God are as wide as mankind.

The same claim also emerges in Paul's use of the Greek word *ecclēsia*. In the Greek Old Testament *ecclēsia* had been regularly used to translate the Hebrew *qahal*, the word for the gathered People of God. By calling themselves God's *ecclēsia* the first Christians avowed their claim to be the true People of God. Sometimes (as in I Cor. 10.32) Paul talks of 'the *ecclēsia* of God'; oftener (as in I Cor. 11.16) he talks, in the plural, of 'the *ecclēsiae* of God'. Sometimes (as in Ephesians) he means the whole number of Christians when he says *ecclēsia*; oftener he refers to the local congregation, adding the word 'Corinth' or 'Thessalonica'. Which came first—the Church (with a capital C) or the churches? Once it was thought that in the beginning there arose local churches which later combined to form the Church. Now we realize that 'the Church was one before it was many'. In other words, the 'Big' Church did not begin with a confederation of local churches; rather the founding of each new local congregation meant one more manifestation of the whole Church. What we have in Paul is this one Church of Christ put down here and there, looking out, as it were, in Corinth or Galatia or Thessalonica. Each local congregation is a station, or outcrop, of *the Ecclēsia*, the one great company of God's People who worship him through Christ in the power of the Holy Spirit.

St Paul's most characteristic name for the Church is the Body of Christ. (See Rom. 12.4ff.; I Cor. 12.12ff.; Col. 1.18, 24, 2.19; and Ephesians *passim*.) This title, defining the Church in terms of Christ, shows that Paul's ecclesiology is a branch of his Christology.

We cannot be sure whence he took the name. One guess is that he was adapting an older Stoic use of the word *sōma* to describe a commonwealth. Another suggestion finds its origin in rabbinical speculation about the body of Adam which was held to include all mankind. (Since Paul thought of the new humanity as incorporated in Christ, may he not have thought of the Church as the body of the Second Adam?) But the most attractive guess derives it from the imagery of the Eucharist in which Christians are 'one body' by partaking of the one loaf symbolizing Christ's body. 'Because there is one loaf,' says Paul, 'we, many as we are, are one body; for it is one loaf of which we all partake' (I Cor. 10.17, NEB).

Doubtless the Hebrew concept of corporate personality helped Paul to think along these lines. (Acts 9.4, 'Saul, Saul, why persecutest thou me?', indicates the solidarity between the risen Christ and his people. Said Augustine, 'The head was lifting up his voice for the members.') To understand Paul's teaching, we have to remember not only that a man's body is the instrument whereby he communicates with the external world, but also that the early Christians had a vivid sense of the living Christ working in their community through the Spirit. So Paul conceived of the Church as the Body of the Risen Lord—a social organism made up of many members, indwelt by the risen Christ, and carrying out his purposes in the world as once his physical body had done in Galilee and Judea.

As Paul works out his theology of the Body, it has both a vertical and a horizontal reference. On the one hand—and we find this only in Colossians and Ephesians[1]—the Body looks up to Christ as its Head and Saviour (Col. 1.18; Eph. 1.22) from whom it draws its vitality (Col. 2.19; Eph. 4.16). On the other hand, those who are in Christ's Body are members one of the other, with gifts which vary but are all needed for the good of the whole (Rom. 12.4ff.; I Cor. 12.12ff.).

The depth and richness of this doctrine is clear. It stresses the headship of Christ, whilst emphasizing the closeness of his union with believers, and their unity in him. It brings out their interdependence. And it finely sets forth the Church's vocation—a vocation magnificently elaborated in Ephesians —as the organism which is to carry out Christ's purposes in the world.

IV

The doctrine of the Church as the Body of Christ leads on to the sacrament of the Lord's Supper in which it was symbolized.

When Paul declares that he received the tradition of the Supper's institution 'from the Lord' (I Cor. 11.23), he is not referring to any visionary experience. The story of what happened at the original Lord's Supper formed part of the apostolic tradition. It went back to the Lord himself, and Paul had received it through those who were actually present.[2]

---

[1] The description of Christ as the Head of the Body is only the application of the idea of the *Kyrios* to the figure of the Body of Christ.

[2] Cf. Cullmann, *The Early Church* (London, 1956), 62, '*From the Lord* points not only to the historical Jesus but to the exalted Lord as the real author of the Church's tradition.'

The sacrament is 'the supernatural food and drink' of the new life (I Cor. 10.3). As Baptism was the sacrament of initiation, so the Supper was the sacrament of continuing fellowship.

Our sources (I Cor. 10.1-4, 14-22, 11.17-33), puzzling though they are in detail, show us that Paul regarded the Supper as a sacrament with three aspects.

First, it *looked back* to 'the night in which he was betrayed'. To celebrate it was to 'proclaim the Lord's death' and to do so in obedience to his command, 'This do as a memorial of me.' Here we must never forget the biblical conception of 'memory'. To remember something in Hebrew fashion is not merely to entertain a pale and static idea of it; it is to make the past event present again, for good or evil. And therefore to 'remember' Christ and his death at the Supper is to make the living Lord present again in the power of his accepted sacrifice.

But if the Supper looked back it also *looked forward* to Christ's coming in glory at the End. At the Last Supper Jesus had declared that he would no more drink of the fruit of the vine till he drank it new in the Kingdom of God (Mark 14.25). Paul's 'until he comes' (I Cor. 11.26) preserves his Lord's eschatological forward-look. The Supper is therefore the Christian's *viaticum* 'between the times'.

But, third, the Supper is itself a *koinōnia* or communion. 'When we bless "the cup of blessing", is it not a means of sharing (*koinōnia*) in the blood of Christ? When we break the bread, is it not a means of sharing (*koinōnia*) in the body of Christ?' (I Cor. 10.16, NEB).

The root idea of *koinōnia* is not so much that of association with other persons—a mere 'togetherness'—as that of sharing in something in which others also share. What is the something here? First, it is 'the blood of Christ'—a vivid metaphor for his redemptive death. Second, it is 'the body of Christ'. This, because it seems to echo the words of the 'tradition', is usually taken to mean his body or person broken for us; but a reference to Christ's 'mystical' Body, the Church, is not impossible in view of what Paul goes on to say: 'Because there is one loaf, we, many as we are, are one body; for it is one loaf of which we all partake' (I Cor. 10.17, NEB).

In any case, Paul's broad meaning is clear. When Christians partake of this food and drink, there is set up the closest fellowship with the Saviour and with one another. The risen Lord, unseen but not unknown, is present with his people, and the worshippers share in the virtue of what he has done for them. When we recall that at the Last Supper Jesus not only connected the broken bread and the red wine with his death for 'the many', but, by inviting his disciples to eat and drink, gave them a share in the atoning power of that death, we may fairly conclude that Paul here, as elsewhere, has faithfully preserved 'the mind of Christ'.

v

Truth for Paul was always 'truth in order to goodness'. The new life, which is salvation as a present experience, is nothing if not moral, and it stands to the Gospel as the fruit to the root. If Paul pitches the ethical requirements of Christianity pretty high, the things required are required as tokens of salvation, not as conditions. A Jewish rabbi might have said: 'If you do not live rightly, you will not be saved.' Paul said, 'If you do not live rightly, you have not been saved.'[1]

The place of ethics in Paul's Christianity is clearly to be

[1] T. W. Manson, *On Paul and John* (London, 1963), 79.

seen in Romans. Omit for the moment chapters 9-11—which may have been composed earlier and separately[1]—and the contents of the letter can be analysed thus:

| | |
|---|---|
| 1.18-3.20 | The Sin of Man |
| 3.21-8.39 | But the Grace of God |
| 12.1-15.13 | Therefore the Christian Ethic |

Paul, of course, does not talk about 'the Christian ethic', nor is he a systematic moralist after the Greek fashion, compiling lists of cardinal virtues or discussing 'the good'. (His nearest equivalent is his list of the nine fruits of the Spirit in Gal. 5.22.) Yet from his exposition of the Christian way of life in his letters we may outline his Christian ethic.

Erskine of Linlathen once wrote:[2] 'In the New Testament religion is grace, and ethics is gratitude.' True of the gospels, it is still more obviously true of Paul. For Paul 'gratitude is the correlative of grace' and upon this gratitude his ethic is grounded. Christian morality is our response in Christian living to the wonderful kindness of God to sinners in Christ. Paul's language varies. In Phil. 1.27 it is, 'Let your manner of life be worthy of the Gospel of Christ'; in Eph. 4.1, 'I beg you to lead a life worthy of your calling'; and in Col. 3.1, 'If you then are risen with Christ, seek the things that are above.' But always it is seen as the right response to 'the extravagant goodness of God' in Christ which is grace. Indeed the response is seen as a kind of *noblesse oblige*. Spiritual rank imposes obligations. Christians are called and challenged to 'live up to' their new status as recipients of God's mercy (Rom. 12.1). In short, for Paul Christian goodness is 'grace' goodness.

Next, for Paul good conduct is not conformity to a code (as it was for the Jewish legalist) but 'a harvest of the Spirit'

[1] C. H. Dodd, *Romans* (London, 1932), xxx.
[2] *Letters of Thomas Erskine*, 16.

(Gal. 5.22), i.e. the spontaneous reaction of the Christian man, under the Spirit's influence, to the successive situations in which he finds himself. 'We are discharged from the law,' he says, 'to serve God in a new way, the way of the spirit, in contrast to the old way, the way of a written code' (Rom. 7.6). The Christian life is, therefore, one of freedom from the law as an external code; for external controls are off and internal ones—those of the Spirit—are on. Yet if 'Christ set us free, to be free men' (Gal. 5.1), rescuing us from the old slavery to the Law, there are limits to the Christian's freedom. If 'all things are permitted' yet every Christian is to 'seek not his own good but that of others' (Phil. 1.24): in other words—and Paul never tires of stressing this—he is to act responsibly as a member of Christ's Body, and love must always have priority over liberty. So Paul could write on the vexed question of eating meat which had once been sacrificed in some heathen temple: 'If food be the downfall of my brother, I will never eat meat any more, for I will not be the cause of my brother's downfall' (I Cor. 8.13, NEB).

But if for Paul Christianity was not a moral code but a life in the Spirit, this does not mean that it had no standards. On the contrary, it has both pattern and principles. The pattern can be put in three words: 'according to Christ' (Col. 2.8): it derives its law and impulse from the whole new Fact of Christ. And this pattern involves principles of Christian action.

An obvious one is the imitation of Christ. In three passages Paul bids his readers copy Christ. In Rom. 15.3 we are told that 'Christ did not please himself'. No more should we. In II Cor. 8.9, urging the Corinthians to be generous, he says, 'You know how generous our Lord Jesus has been; he was rich, yet for your sake he became poor' (NEB). And in Phil. 2.5 the self-denial of Christ becomes a model for Paul's readers: 'Have this mind amongst yourselves which you have in Christ Jesus'—the Christ who renounced 'the form of God' to become a servant and die. (In I Cor. 11.1 and Phil. 3.17 Paul bids his readers imitate himself. Now, though Paul was no 'shrinking violet', this is not egotism. He could not say 'Read your Gospels and imitate Christ.' There were none. What he can and does say is: 'Follow my example, as I follow Christ's.')

Another such principle is obedience to 'the law of Christ' (Gal. 6.2; I Cor. 9.21). But surely (we say) grace and law are for Paul irreconcilable opposites ('You are not under law but under grace', Rom. 6.14)? It is of course true that for Paul man is saved by grace, not by works of law. Nonetheless (as percipient modern scholars have noted) there is a 'nomic' element in his Christianity. Not only does he quote 'commandments' of Christ to settle moral problems (as in I Cor. 7.10 and 9.14), but he weaves the sayings of Jesus into his ethical exhortations (Rom. 12-14 contains no less than eight examples). In other words, Paul found in the moral teaching of Jesus what he called 'the law of Christ', that is to say, an authoritative moral directive or design for Christian living.

But the supreme principle of Christian behaviour is of course *agapē*.

How to translate it is a problem. In a world where 'charity' has almost become 'a dirty word' and 'love' can cover almost everything from Hollywood to heaven, 'caring' perhaps is least inadequate. But the meaning of *agapē* is not in doubt. As *erōs* in Greek is the love which passionately desires and, at its lowest, lusts, and *philia* means friendship, mutual affection between kindred spirits, so *agapē* is the love which seeks not to possess but to give. It is self-spending love.

*Agapē* indeed is not one virtue among many others but a totally new impulse divinely implanted. It is 'God's love in

Christ, reflected and responded to'.[1] Behind it lies Christian experience. In Christ and his Cross Paul had seen a once-for-all demonstration of God's love to undeserving men (Rom. 5.8). With God's saving act in Christ love had invaded our world as never before. Poured into our hearts by God's Spirit (Rom. 5.5), it constrained and controlled men, producing in them a new way of living for God and for their fellow-men: the way of *agapē*.

So, like his Lord, Paul made love the master-key of morals. Writing to the Christians in Rome, he called it 'the fulfilment of the Law' (Rom. 13.10), because anyone who really cares for his neighbour will never dream of injuring him by killing him, or stealing from him, by coveting or by adultery. Failures in the Church at Corinth he traced to a failure of *agapē*. 'Knowledge puffs up,' he said, 'but love builds up' (I Cor. 8.1). 'Above all,' he told the Colossians, 'put on love which is the perfect link' (Col. 3.14). 'Be rooted and grounded in love,' was his counsel to the 'Ephesians' (Eph. 3.17). In fine, love was the greatest of the Spirit's gifts; and in his most famous chapter, his Song of Songs in praise of *agapē*, he sang the necessity, nature and never-failingness of love.

Such an outline is the Pauline ethic. It may be summarized thus:

1. Act as Christ did.
2. Act as Christ directed.
3. Act as members of Christ's Body.
4. Act in *agapē*.

Finally, a word on what we may call Paul's social ethics.

The emergence of specific moral problems in his churches, notably at Corinth, compelled the apostle to give specific

[1] C. F. D. Moule, *The Birth of the New Testament* (London, 1962), 140.

advices and directions. Sometimes in these judgments Paul appears as a man of his time: for example, in I Cor. 11.1-16 he more or less says that this is 'a man's world', and God meant it to be so. But oftener he commands our admiration by his sanctified common sense. The special problems he handles may be temporary and ephemeral; but the principles he lays down for their solution are of abiding value. Let us briefly note what he has to say about the family, woman, marriage, slavery and the State.

In several letters he lays down 'household rules' to regulate relations between husbands and wives, parents and children, masters and slaves. Much of this probably came from the common apostolic *catechēsis*—a body of ethical material drawn from Hellenistic Judaism, but suitably Christianized and reinforced, as we can see in Rom. 12-14, by the moral teaching of Jesus, 'the law of Christ'.

In his view of woman Paul sometimes hardly rises above the contemporary evaluation of her as 'an inferior being'—witness I Cor. 11.3, 9 and Eph. 5.23. But Gal. 3.28 shows that he knew where the logic of the Faith ought to lead him: 'There is no such thing as Jew and Greek, slave and freeman, male and female; for you are all one person in Christ Jesus.' Critics have said that in I Cor. 7 ('It is a good thing,' he says of the unmarried and widows, 'if they stay as I am myself; but if they cannot control themselves, they should marry') he regards marriage as very much 'a second best'. This is fair enough, but we shall do well to hold Paul to his more human and truly Christian teaching in Eph. 5.21-23 where 'the pure love of a man and a woman is a sacrament of the divine love of Christ, and the marriage relation which it consecrates is indissoluble'.[1]

It has often been complained that he leaves the institution

[1] C. H. Dodd, *The Meaning of Paul for Today* (London, 1920), 150.

of slavery uncriticized. To this we may reply that in a society where the Christians had no vote, an attack on the institution as such would have had no effect. On the other hand, we may note that Paul demands a fair deal for the slave from his master ('Masters, be just and fair to your slaves, knowing that you too have a Master in heaven', Col. 4.1) and his handling of the problem of the runaway Onesimus points the way to the true Christian solution. 'Take him back,' he bids Philemon, 'no longer as a slave, but as more than a slave— as a dear brother' (Philemon 16).

Lastly, in one passage he enunciates the Christians' attitude to the State (Rom. 13.1-7). Christians are to be subject to the civil authorities and to pay their taxes. As the powerful ally of the law-abiding man, and the foe of the anti-social person, the civil authorities perform the will of God and can be described as divinely ordained, 'God's agents working for your good'.

# 4

## SALVATION AS A FUTURE HOPE

TO BE a Christian, Brunner has said,[1] is to share something which has happened, which is happening, and which will happen. Our concern now is with what is going to happen, with the consummation of the new life of the man 'in Christ'.

What did Paul teach about the Last Things?

Eschatology in plenty there is in his letters, but no single, unvarying scheme with the time-table of future events finally fixed or the geography of heaven precisely charted. In fact, it can be shown[2] that with the passing years and growing Christian experience and reflection Paul's insight in these matters developed and deepened. What strikes us in his earliest letters, I and II Thessalonians, is his debt to Jewish apocalyptic ideas (such as we find in II Esdras) and his hope of a speedy and dramatic Second Coming of Christ. In the later letters—II Corinthians perhaps marking the dividing line—while the hope of Christ's Coming remains, Paul dwells more and more on the divine blessings which the Christian already possesses. If we compare I and II Thessalonians with, say, Romans and Colossians, we may note the difference. In the Thessalonian letters the stress falls strongly on the impending crisis, and Paul's picture of Christ's Advent—the sounding trumpet, the archangel's voice, the flaming fire—is painted in the conventional colours of Jewish apocalyptic. In Romans and Colossians, however,

[1] *Man in Revolt* (London, 1939), 494.
[2] C. H. Dodd, *New Testament Studies* (Manchester, 1953), 108-28.

there is a decreasing emphasis on the Advent's imminence plus an increasing emphasis on the eternal life to be had here and now in communion with Christ. Along with this we find a new valuation of the natural order. Whereas in the earlier letters—and this is true of I Corinthians also—the present scheme of things is evil and transient, in the later letters Paul recognizes natural human goodness and sets a positive value on human institutions like the State and the family.

Yet though Paul's eschatological thinking thus developed and he never systematized it, he none the less held certain clear and large convictions about God's last purposes for the redeemed.

I

Our first point must be that for Paul, as for all the early Christians, the Last Things were in a true sense already here in human experience. With the Resurrection of Christ the World (or Age) to Come has dawned. Christ has died and risen inaugurating God's New Order, and now at the right hand of God reigns over the Church and the world, albeit his is a hidden kingship. The future has in a real sense become present. In principle, Christians have already begun to enter on their glorious inheritance. They are already 'translated out of the kingdom of darkness into the kingdom of God's dear Son'. Already they have been 'justified' and need not wait for God's verdict on Judgment Day. Already they possess the Holy Spirit promised for the Last Days, and it is the pledge of full salvation. To be sure, they are still 'in the flesh', and are summoned to 'work out their own salvation with fear and trembling', striving against all the powers of evil still active in the world; but their sense of peace with God, their faith-union with the risen and regnant

Christ, and the fruits of the Spirit are sure tokens that they are already experiencing the blessings of the Kingdom which has come with the coming of Christ.

This is what is known as 'realized'—or, better, 'inaugurated'—eschatology.

II

But Paul's theology is far from being all 'realized'. What had happened through God's saving action in Christ was but prelude and pledge of something yet more glorious. If D-Day had dawned, V-Day—the Day of God's final victory—was assured. Amid all awareness of present blessing, there shone for Paul the hope of the day of final redemption—'the Day of Christ' or, as he often calls it, the *Parousia*[1] or 'royal coming' of the Lord.

When would it happen? In his earlier letters (see I Thess. 4.15 and I Cor. 15.51), Paul evidently believed it would happen within his life-time. In his later ones, the consummation is still awaited, but the urgency has gone, and Paul does not now expect to live to see it (II Cor. 5.1; Phil. 1.23).

What would happen after the Lord's Coming? According to some scholars, Paul held that after Christ's *Parousia* there would be a preliminary Messianic Kingdom before the general Resurrection and Judgment. But there are strong reasons[2] for rejecting this view. In any case, it is hard to reconcile with his basic conviction that with Christ's triumph over death the Age to Come had already broken into this

[1] In the papyri *Parousia* is used of the visit of a royal personage to a part of his dominions.
[2] Here are two: (1) In the only place where Paul expressly mentions the Kingdom of Christ it is present fact (Col. 1.13); (2) when Paul speaks of a Kingdom in the future, it is the kingdom *of God*, and one that knows no end (e.g. I Cor. 15.50; II Thess. 1.5).

one and Jesus himself was now not only risen but reigning. In fact, Paul's eschatology was far simpler. He believed that the Coming of Christ would be followed by the Resurrection and the Judgment which would usher in the final Consummation when God would be all in all (I Cor. 15.20-28).

What would this final act of God in Christ involve? First and obviously, Judgment. 'God', says Paul, 'shall judge the secrets of men by Jesus Christ' (Rom. 2.16). (In Rom. 14.10 he speaks of God's judgment seat, in II Cor. 5. 10 of Christ's.) Only now 'there is no condemnation for those who are in (united with) Christ Jesus' (Rom. 8.1): the Christian, already 'acquitted' by God's grace, may face the final Assize with assurance.

Second, Paul's concept of final salvation is indefeasibly social. It is a fellowship of redeemed persons in the eternal Kingdom of God, with Christ 'the eldest among a large family of brothers' (Rom. 8.29, NEB). And in one passage —Rom. 8.18-25—his hope embraces not only the sons of God but the renewal of the whole creation.

Third, the *Parousia* will mean the open triumph of Christ and his saints (Col. 3.4), i.e. the revealing of the hidden-ness of the Easter victory, and the final defeat of all evil powers in the world, including death itself (I Cor. 15.26).

III

This leads to the third main point in Paul's eschatology. The heart of the Christian Hope can be put in three words, 'being with Christ'.

Christ, the first-born among many brethren, is already risen and reigning. He is 'the first-fruits'. What happened to him will happen to those who are his; for we are 'joint-heirs with Christ', and 'if we have died with him, we believe that we shall also live with him' (Rom. 6.8). 'So shall we be always with the Lord' (I Thess. 4.17). And this hope, it must be added, is not only of being with Christ, but of being *like* him, since the Christian's destiny is to 'be shaped to the likeness of God's Son' (Rom. 8.29; cf. I John 3.2).

If the heart of the Christian Hope is being with Christ, the secret of it is to be 'in Christ' now. 'As in Adam all die,' Paul declares, 'so in Christ shall all be made alive' (I Cor. 15.22). This surely means: 'As all that are in Adam die, so all that are in Christ will be made alive' (cf. I Thess. 4.16). But what of those who are not only not 'in Christ' but have even rejected him (as many of his compatriots had)?[1] In II Thess. 1.9 Paul takes a sombre view: 'They will suffer the punishment of eternal ruin, cut off from the presence of the Lord' (NEB). Yet when he comes to write Romans, reluctant to believe that 'his kinsmen according to the flesh' will be finally lost, he moves to some kind of 'larger hope' (Rom. 11.32)—a view which widens still further in Colossians where God's purpose, according to Paul, is 'to reconcile to himself all things, whether in earth or heaven' (Col. 1.20; Eph. 1.10).

Yet it would be hazardous, on the strength of Paul's words in Rom. 11.32 about God having 'mercy upon all', to conclude that the apostle was a 'universalist' in the modern sense of the word. In Rom. 11 he is thinking of races, not of individuals, and elsewhere he distinguishes between those who are being 'saved' and those who are 'perishing' (II Cor. 2.13f.). To find in Paul's words the dogmatic assertion that every man, no matter what his sins, will finally receive mercy and reach God's eternal Kingdom is to say something which is probably not true of Paul and certainly not true of the rest of the New Testament.

[1] In I Thess. 2.16 Paul declares that the wrath of God has fallen on the Jews 'finally' or 'for good and all'.

IV

The mode of the Christian's heavenly life is 'a spiritual body' (I Cor. 15.35ff.; II Cor. 5.1ff.; Phil. 3.20f.).

Paul holds that the life to come is a gift of God, not (as the Greeks held) a natural possession of man. He also insists (as a good Jew) on the 'embodied' nature of the resurrection life. Not the immortality of the soul but the resurrection of the body is his concern and hope. But when he uses the word 'body' (*sōma*), he is not hoping for a revivification of our physical make-up—a resurrection of relics. 'Flesh and blood,' he says, 'cannot inherit the (eternal) kingdom of God' (I Cor. 15.50). For Paul the body is the principle of identity which persists through all changes of substance—'organism' or 'person' would perhaps give his meaning. Now the body has a material means of expression suited to this earthly sphere; hereafter God will give it a new embodiment befitting the heavenly world—a body of glory, a spirit-body. Our lowly bodies will be changed to resemble Christ's glorious body (Phil. 3.21)—the body invested with the glory of another world which Paul had seen on the Damascus Road. 'As we have worn the likeness of the man of dust, so we shall wear the likeness of the heavenly man' (I Cor. 15.49, NEB).

Of Paul's teaching we may say two things. First, it assures us that the personality is renewed in the future life not as a ghost but with all that is needed for its self-expression and power to communicate with others. Second, it avoids the drawbacks of both the Greek and the popular Jewish view. The Greek doctrine of the immortality of the disembodied soul secured spirituality but endangered personal identity. The Jewish doctrine of an 'embodied' life, conceived as it was mostly in 'fleshly' terms, preserved identity but imperilled spirituality.

When does the great change take place? When Paul is writing I Corinthians, his answer is, 'At Christ's Parousia' (I Cor. 15.51f.). But when he comes to write II Corinthians he has himself been very near the gates of death (II Cor. 1.8) and has thought more seriously about what happens after it. Now he answers, 'At death'.[1] 'For we know that if the earthly tent we live in is destroyed, we have a building from God, a house not made with hands, eternal in the heavens' (II Cor. 5.1. Paul seems here to be echoing the saying attributed to Jesus at his trial, Mark 14.58. The false witnesses made it refer to the destruction of the Temple. According to John 2.19ff. it was a promise of his Resurrection). (We may add that in Phil. 1.23 Paul's clear conviction is that death will usher him—whether 'bodied' or 'disembodied'—into the presence of his Lord.) The fact that Paul now believed that Christians would receive their spiritual bodies at death, and need not wait for them to the last Day, does not mean that the Parousia had lost its significance for him. Rather, only at the Parousia would the work of Christ in his Body be perfected, only then would the sons of God be manifested in glory (Rom. 8.19, 21; Col. 3.4).

In his teaching about the Last Things Paul is aware that 'we know only in part', that our present knowledge is very much like vision through an unclear mirror. That complete redemption awaits all those who are 'in Christ' he is sure, as that God will finally 'be all in all'. Beyond this he does not go. A strong faith, it has been said, is not curious about details. It is enough to know that 'this perishable nature must put on the imperishable, and this mortal nature must put on immortality' (I Cor. 15.53). For the rest, 'eye hath not seen, nor ear heard, neither have entered into the heart of

[1] So Charles, Dodd, Bultmann, Davies, etc. On the whole passage see R. F. Hettlinger's excellent discussion in *The Scottish Journal of Theology* for June 1957.

man, the things which God hath prepared for them that love him' (I Cor. 2.9).

### NOTE ON SŌMA

For the Greeks, *sōma*, *sēma*, 'the body is a tomb'; for Paul, the *sōma* is the vehicle of the resurrection.

*Sōma*, in Paul, can of course mean a physical body (as in I. Cor. 13.3); but in many passages the word stands for the whole man, the self, the personality, and can be translated by a personal pronoun. Thus in Phil 1.20 'in my body' means 'in my person', 'in me'; and when Paul says 'present your bodies as a living sacrifice' (Rom. 12.1) he means 'offer yourselves'.

*Sōma*, because it stands for man as a being in the world, is subject to the powers which corrupt our life—sin and death. Consequently if Paul can speak of 'flesh of sin', i.e. sinful flesh (Rom. 8.3), he can equally speak of a 'body of sin' (Rom. 6.6), i.e. a sinful self.

But, though both words are grounded in the Hebrew *basar*, 'body' and 'flesh' are not for Paul synonyms. Both words stand indeed for the whole man, but man as seen from two different angles. *Sarx* is man as doomed to perish; *sōma* is man as destined for God. For 'the body is for the Lord, and the Lord for the body', and its destiny is resurrection (I Cor. 6.13f.). Only, as Paul teaches in I Cor. 15, the physical body must be 'changed' by God into a 'spiritual' one, if it is to be fit for the heavenly life.

# 5

# THE SAVIOUR

WE have outlined Paul's doctrine of salvation. Its source was God, its mediator Christ. 'For us', he says, 'there is one God the Father, from whom are all things and for whom we exist, and one Lord Jesus Christ through whom are all things and through whom we exist' (I Cor. 8.6). Our final question is, therefore, How did Paul conceive of the Saviour? (The title, incidentally, is used by Paul only in Phil. 3.20 and Eph. 5. 23. An OT title of God—see, for example, Isa. 43.3, 11 —it was commonly applied in Paul's day to earthly rulers and emperors. There even exists an inscription in which Nero is hailed as 'the saviour of the world'. Here perhaps we may find the reason why Paul uses it so rarely.)

Before we attempt an answer, there are two prior questions to be asked. The first is, How much did Paul know of what we call 'the Jesus of history'?

It is often said, quite wrongly, that Paul knew next to nothing about him. When this question is discussed, we need to bear in mind three things: (1) The Epistles are Epistles, not Gospels, and do not set out to recount 'all that Jesus began to do and to teach' (Acts 1.1, referring to Luke's Gospel); (2) Paul numbered among his acquaintances men like Peter, John and James the Lord's brother who had known Jesus in 'the days of his flesh' and could correct or supplement that knowledge of Jesus which Paul must have had even before his conversion;[1] and (3) Paul's gaze was,

---

[1] When Paul wrote Colossians and Philemon, both our second and third evangelists—Mark and Luke—were with him.

naturally enough, fixed on the living and exalted Lord. (For us 'the life of Christ' means the earthly career of Jesus. For Paul—see Rom. 5.10—it was not the life preceding his death which was primary, but the life which followed it, the life of the risen Son of God.)

Yet, in fact, we can glean enough from his letters to write what Renan called 'a brief life of Christ'. Let this summary suffice.

Born of a woman (Gal. 4.4) and descended from David (Rom. 1.3), his earthly lot was that of a poor man (II Cor. 8.9). He had brothers, one of them called James (I Cor. 9.5;[1] Gal. 1.19). His ministry was to the Jews (Rom. 15.8) and he had apostles, known as 'the Twelve' (I Cor. 15.4), two of them being Cephas and John (Gal. 2.9). Before the Jews killed him (I Thess. 2.15)—indeed 'on the night in which he was betrayed'[2] (I Cor. 11.23)—he instituted the Lord's Supper (I Cor. 11.23ff.). He was crucified and buried, and on the third day was raised and appeared to many witnesses (I Cor. 15.3ff.).

Nor is Paul ignorant of Jesus' *character*. He was 'gentle and magnanimous' (II Cor. 10.1; cf. Matt. 11.29); obedient to his Father's will (Rom. 5.19; Phil. 2.8); of a steadfast endurance (II Thess. 3.5); and unacquainted with sin (II Cor. 5.21). And when in I Cor. 13.4-7 Paul limns the features of *agapē*, can we doubt who it was sat in the studio of his imagination for that portrait? (As in George Herbert's poem 'Love bade me welcome', we might for 'Love' write 'Christ'.)

As for Christ's *teaching*, Paul can quote, when need demands it, sayings of the Lord (I Cor. 7.10, 9.14, 11.23ff.; and Acts 20.35). Elsewhere—see especially Rom. 12-14 and I Thess. 5—Paul's own teaching unmistakably echoes his Lord's at point after point: on non-resistance to evil (Rom.

[1] I Cor. 9.5 corroborates Mark 1.30 (Peter was married).
[2] Paul's 'betrayed' suggests he knew the story of Judas.

12.17; I Thess. 5.15; cf. Matt. 5.39f.); and returning blessing for cursing (Rom. 12.14; cf. Matt. 5.44); on love as the Law's fulfilment (Rom. 13.8f.; Mark 12.28-34); on the need to restore an erring brother (Gal. 6.1; Matt. 18.15ff.); and the duty of 'rendering to all their dues' (Rom. 13.7; Mark 12.13-17); on sins of censorious judgment (Rom. 14.4, 10; Matt. 7.1) and causing others to stumble (Rom. 14.13; Matt. 18.6ff.); on freedom from worry (Phil. 4.6; Matt. 6.25), and being at once simple and wise (Rom. 16.19; Matt. 10.16), and mountain-moving faith (I Cor. 13.2; Matt. 17.20).

The list is not exhaustive; and we could have thrown in, for good measure, an 'unfamiliar saying' of Jesus (I Thess. 5.21f., quoting an *Agraphon* preserved for us by Clement of Alexandria), a Dominical simile ('The day of the Lord comes like a thief in the night'—an echo of Christ's parable of the Burglar, I Thess. 5.2; Matt. 24.43), and a reference to the first word of the Lord's Prayer (*Abba*, Rom. 8.15; Gal. 4.6; cf. Luke 11.2 and Mark 14.36). But enough has been quoted to show how baseless is the charge that Paul was ignorant of the Jesus of history.

We may now turn to the second question: How is Paul's Christ related to the Christ of the Synoptic Gospels?

Fifty years ago, when theological Liberalism was in the ascendancy, the charge was often made that Paul had turned the present-preacher of God's Fatherhood into a cosmic Redeemer—that between the historic Jesus and the Pauline Christ a great gulf was fixed.

Nowadays no self-respecting scholar lightly levels that charge. The idea is now discredited that 'beneath the surface of the Gospels we can unearth a purely human prophet of the Divine Fatherhood and human brotherhood who was transformed by St Paul into a supernatural Saviour'.[1]

Various factors have led to this result.

---

[1] Alec Vidler, *Christian Belief* (London, 1950), 48.

To begin with, the re-discovery and better understanding of the eschatology of the Gospels has had its effect. Not only has it shown the Liberal picture of Jesus to be false, but it has revealed the Jesus of the Gospels to be an immeasurably greater person than the Liberals had supposed—to be indeed the all-decisive person at a supreme crisis in God's dealings with men.

In the second place, scholars who studied afresh the self-revelation of Jesus in the Gospels (and none did it more convincingly than Denney in *Jesus and the Gospel*) recalled us to one who knew himself to be the Son of God in a unique and lonely sense. We began to see that the Christology of Jesus himself was not unworthy to bear the weight of the claims made for him by St Paul.

And, thirdly, the gulf which had seemed to yawn between Paul and the earliest Christians was well-nigh bridged. We began to perceive how much Paul owed to his Christian predecessors. If Paul set Jesus on the divine side of reality, so did they. If he called Jesus Messiah, Lord and Son of God, no less did they. Paul and the Jerusalem leaders may have clashed on other issues. There is not a scrap of evidence that they ever clashed on the supreme issue of Christology. The Christ Paul preached was the same Christ as his precursors preached. Paul's was a greater Christ only in the sense that Paul interpreted him by new needs, relating him to the religious yearnings not of Judaism only but of the great Gentile world which he was called to evangelize. In short, historic Christianity stems from Jesus, not Paul; but Paul was foremost in grasping the true magnitude of his person and work; and for this all succeeding generations of Christians have been his debtors.

We are ready now to study Paul's view of Christ; but before we consider the titles Paul applies to him, let us set down his doctrine in more general terms.

'Life means Christ to me,' Paul said once (Phil. 1.21). Does this mean that for him Christ has usurped the place of God? No; rather it is God who meets men in Christ, the same God who once acted in creation: 'It is the God who said, "Let light shine out of darkness" who has shone in our hearts to give the light of the knowledge of the glory of God in the face of Christ' (II Cor. 4.6). But this God is only surely accessible to sinful man in Christ. One may know something of God from his creation—glimpse his everlasting power and deity in the things he has made (Rom. 1.20); and one may discern his sovereign will for men in the law; but neither in nature nor in law but only in Christ is God savingly known. For in Christ God of his grace draws near to sinful men and stretches out his saving hand. And this Christ, as Paul's letters testify on every page, is no mere figure in past history but a living and delivering Presence who dwells, by the power of the Spirit, in the believer's heart (Eph. 3.17). This is God's great secret, as Paul tells the Colossians (1.27): 'Christ in you, the hope of glory.'

Of this Christ, crucified, risen and regnant, Paul is the herald and ambassador; yet his 'Christophory' implies a 'Christology', and we must now sum it up.

Paul affirms the full humanity of Christ: 'born of a woman, born under the law' (Gal. 4.4): 'For as by a man came death, by a man came also the resurrection of the dead' (I Cor. 15.21): Christ came 'in the likeness of sinful flesh' (Rom. 8.3), i.e. in that nature which is in us identified with sin.[1] No less certainly, however, Paul sets him on the divine side of reality, conjoining his name with the name of God at point after point. Once indeed he seems to call him 'God' (Rom. 9.5); yet if this interpretation (favoured by the

---

[1] 'Paul wishes to say that the humanity of Christ was like our own, except that in his flesh sin had no place.' V. Taylor, *The Person of Christ in New Testament Teaching* (London, 1958), 40.

Fathers) is now rejected as it often is (see the RSV and the NEB), Paul makes claims for Christ hardly less exalted. He is the God-man: 'in him dwells the plenitude of deity corporately' (*sōmatikōs*, i.e. in one organism or personality, Col. 2.9). If he subordinates Christ to God the Father—'the head of Christ is God' (I Cor. 11.3; cf. I Cor. 3.23 and 15.28) —he does not scruple to apply to him titles and words used in the Old Testament of the All Highest (Rom. 10.13; I Cor. 1.2). He conceives of Christ as having pre-existed (I Cor. 10.4; Gal. 4.4; Phil. 2.6). He links Christ with the Holy Spirit, and though probably not identifying them, he can say of Christ, 'The last Adam became a life-giving Spirit' (I Cor. 15.45; cf. II Cor. 3.17). But perhaps the most staggering claim he makes is when he assigns Christ a *cosmic* role. 'For us there is one Lord Jesus Christ, through whom are all things and through whom we exist' (I Cor. 8.6). And if we are tempted to judge this as a mere *obiter dictum* to the Corinthians, not to be taken too seriously, we are prevented by Col. 1.15-18, where Paul, in face of the Colossian 'theosophists' who were busy scaling down his significance, gives Christ the freedom of the universe and depicts him as creation's goal:

He is the image of the invisible God; his is the primacy over all created things. In him everything in heaven and on earth was created, not only things visible but also the invisible orders of thrones, sovereignties, authorities and powers: the whole universe has been created through him and for him. And he exists before everything, and all things are held together in him (NEB).

The man who wrote these words believed that embedded in the constitution of creation itself was a reference to the Person and Sovereignty of Christ.

After all this any enumeration of the titles Paul applies to Jesus may seem almost unnecessary.

From the day of his conversion Paul had no doubt that Jesus was the promised *Messiah*. 'Paul', we read in Acts 9.22, 'silenced the Jews of Damascus with his cogent proofs that Jesus was the Messiah' (NEB).

How comes it, then, that there is so little of this in his letters? Never once does he say in so many words 'Jesus is the Messiah', and the word 'Christ' has almost become for Paul, as it is for us today, a proper name, not a title. Nonetheless, in a few passages—notably Rom. 9.5 ('from them, in natural descent, sprang the Messiah', NEB; cf. Col. 2.6)—the titular sense lingers on; and in fact, as Dahl[1] has shown, Paul's whole work as an apostle was conditioned by the Messiahship of Jesus.

Why does Paul not labour the proof of Jesus' Messiahship in his letters? First and obviously, because he was pre-eminently the apostle to the Gentiles, and the word 'Messiah' would have conveyed as much—or as little—to them as the word 'Mahdi' conveys to English audiences today: and, second, probably because he knew that no racial or traditional categories could confine the Redeemer: he belonged not to Israel only but to all mankind.

If statistics prove anything, Paul's favourite name for the Saviour was '*the Lord*' (*Ho Kyrios*, 222 times in all, if we include combinations like 'the Lord Jesus', etc.). Unlike Messiah, here was a title that was meaningful to Gentiles with 'their gods many and lords many' (I Cor. 8.5) and gave to Jesus an exalted religious significance.

When and how did Jesus come to be so designated? In 'the days of his flesh' the disciples had sometimes addressed him in Aramaic as *Mari*, or 'Lord' (Mark 11.3; Matt. 7.21; John 13.13); but though these passages disclose more than a mere teacher-disciple relationship, this is not the absolute use of the term 'Lord' we find in Paul's letters. That came only

[1] N. A. Dahl in *Studia Paulina*, 94.

after the exaltation of Jesus, and the evidence suggests that it was in the worship of the Aramaic-speaking Church that it first happened.

Consider the little piece of Aramaic preserved for us by Paul in I Cor. 16.22: *Marana tha*. This is a prayer rather than a confession. It means 'Our Lord, come' rather than 'Our Lord comes.' And if we add the evidence of the *Didache* 10.6 to I Cor. 16.22,[1] we infer that *Marana tha* was a prayer used at the earliest eucharists of the Church. It probably meant (as Cullmann[2] suggests) not only 'Come, Lord at the End' (as in Rev. 22.20) but also, 'Come, Lord, now as we gather at this meal.' In any case, when the first Christians called the exalted Jesus *Marana*, it was a term of religious veneration. 'Teacher, come' is an impossible rendering: the phrase can only mean, 'Our Lord, come.'

It was this title which, when the Gospel moved out on to Hellenistic soil, was done into Greek as *Ho Kyrios* 'the Lord' (or 'our Lord'); as *Kyrios Jesus* 'Jesus is Lord' (Rom. 10.9; I Cor. 12.3) became one of the earliest Christian confessions.

To contemporary pagans, wont to bestow the title on their gods and goddesses, *Ho Kyrios* meant much. To Paul and the earliest Christians it meant even more, for in the Septuagint, which was the Bible of the apostolic church, *Ho Kyrios* translated *Adonai* which itself replaced the ineffable name of God himself. Not only did the title set Jesus incontrovertibly on the side of Deity, but it expressed as no other did the conviction that Jesus was now at the right hand of God and interceding for them with the Father. The Lord Jesus was not merely a figure in past history or an object of future hope; he was a living, present reality able to save those who put faith in him, to enter into fellowship with his

[1] Some scholars hold that I Cor. 16.20-24 concern the Eucharist.
[2] *The Christology of the New Testament* (London, 1959), 212.

C

confessors, to bring their prayers before God and make them effective.

Into this title Paul himself poured all the wealth of his devotion. It set forth his own relation to Jesus: Jesus was the Lord; he was his Lord's bond-servant. And the aim of all his apostolic labours was to bring men into a like relationship: 'For we preach not ourselves but Christ Jesus as Lord, and ourselves as your servants for Jesus' sake' (II Cor. 4.5).

Paul had a third great title for Christ. 'I live', he wrote, 'by faith in the son of God who loved me and gave himself for me' (Gal. 2.20). Jesus was *the Son of God*—in a very special sense. In all, Paul uses the title seventeen times: four times it is 'the Son of God', twice 'the Son' and eleven times the more intimate 'His Son' (twice, 'His own Son').[1]

In calling Jesus by this title Paul was doing no new thing. His Christian predecessors had done it before him, as Rom. 1.4 (by wide consent a pre-pauline Christian creed) and other evidence shows. And if we ask why they should have done so, no good reason can be given except that it was known that Jesus had so spoken of himself (Mark 1.11, 12.6, 13.32; Matt. 11.27).

When Paul refers to Christ as 'the Son' or 'His Son' it is generally in the context of God the Father's *redeeming* work. Thus, 'when the time had fully come, God sent forth his Son . . . to redeem' (Gal. 4.4); 'while we were yet enemies, we were reconciled to God by the death of his Son' (Rom. 5.10); 'God sending his own Son in the likeness of sinful flesh and for sin, condemned sin in the flesh' (Rom. 8.3); 'He did not spare his own Son but gave him up for us all' (Rom. 8.32). For God who predestines men to be 'conformed to the image of his Son' (Rom. 8.29), translates them

[1] Why does the title 'Son of God' occur so much more rarely in Paul than 'the Lord'? Probably, as Vincent Taylor has suggested, because 'the Lord' was used in worship, whereas 'the Son' was the important title in teaching. *The Person of Christ*, 44.

'into the kingdom of his dear son' (Col. 1.13), and sends the Spirit of his Son into their hearts (Gal. 4.6).

In such passages Paul uses the name to define Christ's relation to God. It is clearly far more than that of Messiahship; and if we ask what it is, can we do better than say with Anderson Scott that it is something 'personal, ethical and inherent';[1] involving a community of nature, will and purpose? In short, it is a Sonship which we can only call 'unique' and 'unshared'.

These three titles do not exhaust Paul's names for Jesus or the categories he uses to set forth his significance.

Thus in Rom. 5.12-21 and I Cor. 15.21f. and 45ff. he compares Christ with Adam. As Paul thought of Christianity as a new creation, so he thought of Adam and Christ as the inclusive Representatives of the old and new humanities. The fact that we no longer think of Adam as the first human being (but rather as 'Everyman') should not make us miss the point Paul is making, viz., the representative and racial nature of Christ's redemptive work. Paul thinks of Christ as 'Adam in reverse', the second Man who repairs—and more than repairs—the damage wrought by the first one. Thus he stresses the solidarity of the race with Adam in his sin and its consequence, death. If today we should put it differently, we should still mean what Paul means: in virtue of our common fallen humanity—what Paul calls 'the old man' in us—we sin and deserve death. But our salvation is achieved through our solidarity with Christ, the second Adam, in his righteousness and its consequence, life; for we are incorporated by faith and baptism in the new humanity of Christ, which is his Body, the Church.[2]

Again, Paul spoke of Christ as the Divine Wisdom (I Cor.

[1] *Christianity according to St Paul* (Cambridge, 1961), 255.
[2] See Alan Richardson, *A Theological Word-Book of the Bible* (London, 1950), 15.

1.24, 30; Col. 1.15). The ultimate source of this doctrine is
Prov. 8 where Wisdom is conceived as pre-existent and as
God's agent in creation. In using the figure of Wisdom to
express what Christ meant for him, Paul sought to show not
only his belief in Christ's pre-existence (which he asserts
elsewhere) but also his conviction that the created universe
bears the marks of the Saviour and that to live 'according
to Christ' is the natural life.

Finally, though Paul never says in so many words that
Christ is the New Torah, he certainly thought of him so.
'Conformity to Christ, his teaching and life,' writes W. D.
Davies,[1] 'has taken the place for Paul of conformity to the
Jewish Torah. Jesus himself—in word and deed—is a new
Torah.' The proof is in passages like II Cor. 3.7ff. and Rom.
10.6ff. (where Paul takes words from Deut. 30.12ff., originally referring to the Law, and applies them to Christ). When
we remember that for the Jew the *Torah* meant 'all that
God has made known of his nature, purpose and character
and of what he would have men be and do' (Moore), we can
see that Paul regarded Christ as the complete revelation, in
flesh and blood, of God's nature and will for man.

Such titles and categories[2] show how the apostle ran-

[1] *St Paul and Rabbinic Judaism* (London, 1955), 148.
[2] Paul never calls Jesus 'the Servant of the Lord'. Yet in four
passages (Rom. 4.25, 5.19; I Cor. 15.3; and Phil. 2.6-11) he applies
'Servant' language to Christ and his work. Three of the four are
'traditional', i.e. pre-pauline, and in the other one, Rom. 5.19, Paul
may well be combining the two concepts of the Son of Man and the
Servant of the Lord as Jesus himself had done (Mark 10.45).

Now Isaiah's 'Suffering Servant' was (as the *pais theou* passages
in Acts 3.13, 26; 4.27, 30 show) one of the earliest answers to the
question, Who is Jesus? It was also something which, as the Gospels
show, lay deep in the self-consciousness of Jesus. Why did not Paul
make more use of it in his thinking about Christ? Did he think the
phrase with its lowly associations would be offensive to Gentile ears?
Or was it that, while the title adequately described Christ's *earthly*
work, it needed to be supplemented by other titles (like 'the Lord')
if it was to set forth the present activity of the risen Lord?

sacked language and thought to set forth the absolute significance of Christ. In Christ he had found 'unsearchable riches' (Eph. 3.8). In Christ's face he had seen shining the splendour of the Creator of all things (II Cor. 4.6). Through Christ he had gained access to the Father (Eph. 2.18). What wonder, then, if he believed that Christ's story did not begin in a Bethlehem cradle and that he saw the world and history moving on to Christ?

We, Christians of the twentieth century, whose mental world is so different from Paul's, cannot use all Paul's language when we proclaim Christ to men. Thought-forms have changed and concepts intelligible to Paul's contemporaries are alien to our generation. Our task is, using the idioms and categories of our time, to assign Christ the supreme place Paul gave him in the saving purposes of God for us men:

> For all things are yours . . .
> Whether the world, or life, or death,
> Or the present or the future,
> All are yours;
> And you are Christ's, and Christ is God's
>
> (I Cor. 3.21ff.).

# 6

# ON THE WRATH OF GOD AND PREDESTINATION

WHAT has Paul to say about the wrath of God and Pre-destination? These two questions deserve a separate chapter for their discussion.

I

Sixteen times in his letters Paul refers to the wrath of God. Thrice he gives the phrase in full, but generally he speaks of 'the wrath'. He says that God 'shows' wrath, or that his wrath is being revealed against human sin. Sinners are 'vessels of wrath' (or 'children of wrath'). Judgment Day is 'the Day of wrath', as Jesus is our 'deliverer from the wrath to come'.

This language repels many people today. They would fain hold that anger in every shape and form is foreign to God. They would like to interpret Paul's phrase in terms of some impersonal doctrine of retribution—the inevitable operation of the law of cause and effect in a moral world.

But the Bible does not take this way. No student of the Old Testament prophets can doubt that the wrath of God was for them a personal activity of God. Nor can we doubt that, though Jesus laid a new emphasis on the love of God, he found the divine reaction to evil an awful reality, and (we may add) that, as he himself approached death—witness the 'cup' saying and the Cry of Dereliction—felt the weight, without himself being the object of provocation, of the wrath of God.

The same is true of Paul and the other New Testament writers who take a graver view of God's wrath than even the Old Testament prophets. On the other hand, they have found a hope of reconciliation to God unknown to the Old Testament. 'God has not destined us for wrath, but to obtain salvation through our Lord Jesus Christ' (I Thess. 5.9).

We have noted that Paul often speaks of 'the wrath' (it almost demands a capital letter) without naming God. This is not because he thinks of it impersonally, but because he finds it quite unnecessary to say whose wrath it is (cf. the phrase 'the Day' meaning Judgment Day, *Dies illa*). By 'the wrath' Paul means God's holy displeasure at sin. It is the eternal divine reaction against evil without which God would not be the moral Governor of the world. Paul thinks of it as both present and future. It is that divine aversion to evil and sin which, though active in the present time, will not reach its climax till the Judgment.

Loyalty to the Bible will not, then, allow us to jettison the doctrine. But when we think of it, we can remember two things. First, God's wrath is not to be thought of in terms of sinful man's. It is not the emotional reaction of an irritated self-concern, as it is so often with us. We must not picture God as a man who suddenly loses his temper and casts aside his love. Rather, if we use human analogies, should we think of that 'righteous indignation' which a good man feels in the presence of stark evil—and multiply by infinity.

Second: only a sentimentalist theology will find God's wrath incompatible with his love. (The opposite of love is hate, not wrath.) Rather should we conceive God's wrath as the obverse of his love—'the adverse wind', the antagonism, of his holy love to all that is evil. (Luther called God's wrath his 'strange work', as mercy was his 'proper work'.)

Paul found that wrath of God a reality in his day. When men rebel against God (he said) God 'gives them up' to the consequences of their sins, to suffering of body, hardening of their hearts, the complete obfuscation of their spiritual faculties (Rom. 1.18-32). Has this ceased to be true in the twentieth century?

## II

Predestination and Election are two cognate Pauline doctrines not now much in vogue. The average man today, if he believes in God, generally doubts whether God has an eternal plan for men and nations. The word Election smacks to him of Calvinism and ideas of divine sovereignty now, as he supposes, deservedly discredited. If he is a Scot, he has read 'Holy Willie's Prayer' with its scarifying indictment of eighteenth-century Calvinistic conceptions of Election, and he has a vague suspicion that this 'ferocious theology' with its God who sends

'Ane to Heaven an' ten to Hell'

all for his glory goes back behind Calvin and Augustine to the Apostle Paul. What truth is there in this?

St Paul most certainly believed in Election and Predestination. Two brief passages from his letters make this pellucidly clear:

He chose us in him (Christ) before the foundation of the world, that we should be holy and blameless before him. He destined us in love to be his sons through Jesus Christ, according to the purpose of his will (Eph. 1.4f.).

For those whom he foreknew he also predestined to be conformed to the image of his Son, in order that he might be the first-born among many brethren. And those whom he predestined he also called; and those whom he called he also justified; and those whom he justified he also glorified (Rom. 8.29f.).

The man who wrote these words certainly believed not only that God was the supreme Disposer of all things but that he elected from eternity to save some men and predestined them to glory. Is this an absurd and ridiculous belief? Is it not, basically, the conviction that we just do not happen to exist—that our life has its roots in eternity—and that our salvation (if we are conscious of such a thing) begins in the eternal God (as the work of art begins first in the mind of the artist) and is actualized in Christ, the divinely-sent Saviour of men?

But does not Paul go further than this? Indeed he does, in Rom. 9.17-21. Here the problem before him is the Jews' failure to accept Christ and the Gospel, and inevitably he has to discuss the place of free will in the divine purpose. His argument is that, since God is sovereign, he can do as he wills, even with his own chosen People. Unfortunately he so over-drives his argument as to conclude: 'God has mercy upon whomever he wills, and he hardens the heart of whomever he wills.' Were this true, God would come near to being a non-moral despot, like Hardy's 'President of the Immortals'. And, alas, Paul did not improve matters by producing in the next verses his unhappy analogy of the Potter and the clay, in order to silence all cavillers. But in fairness to the Apostle we must add that, if in Rom. 9 Paul says God can make his People 'vessels of wrath', he goes on to say in Rom. 11 that these same vessels of wrath will finally be saved!

The truth is that Paul's doctrine of election crops up as a pure expression of the religious experience of grace. Says Otto:[1]

---

[1] *Das Heilige* (Dodd's translation), 109.

A man who is the object of grace, when he looks back on himself, feels more and more that he has become what he is by no act or activity of his own, that grace came to him without his own will or power, that it took hold of him, drove him, led him on. Before any act of his own, he sees redeeming love seeking and choosing him, and recognizes an eternal decree of grace on his behalf.

This is Paul's experience, and the experience of many since who have known God's grace. The stress falls wholly on the divine initiative of grace in election. But does not Paul also lay great weight on the importance of the human response? Of course he does. Go back to Rom. 9-11. If in chapter 9 Paul implies that God has rejected the Jews, in chapter 10 he argues that they have really by their own unbelief rejected themselves. In all this he is grappling with the ancient problem of the relation of the divine sovereignty to human free will, a problem which, since we lack omniscience, is ultimately as mysterious as the existence of evil in a world made by a good God. Yet, little as we understand the mystery, our best wisdom is to hold *both* convictions, viz. that our salvation is grounded in the eternal will of God, and that such salvation depends upon a man's own response to the grace of God offered him in Christ.

Now let us consider predestination more closely. Did Paul really teach the pernicious doctrine of 'Double Predestination', namely, that God has from all eternity willed that some should be saved, and that some should be reprobated for ever?

The short answer is No. Reprobation is 'the shadow side' of the doctrine of election. But into that shadow side Paul does not peer. Not a word does he say about men being predestined by God to eternal damnation. It is true that to say that some people are eternally elected to salvation implies, in logic, that others are eternally rejected. In logic, Yes; but here Paul is splendidly illogical. What Paul does say is this. The Gospel comes to all men, challenging them to the decision of faith. All hangs on that decision. If Paul speaks of 'perishing' (as he does), it is never of something which simply is. The possibility of it is mentioned in order to evoke faith. He says in effect: 'If you perish, it is your own fault. If you have saving faith, then know that it is a gift of God's grace.' The opposite of election, for Paul, is not predestination to perdition; it is unbelief—a self-incurred thing. And if we draw the logical conclusion of election, as the Calvinists did, then we clash with 'the Gospel within the Gospels'— that God gave Christ that men might not perish but have eternal life (John 3.16). No man may hold that God has eternally predestined even one soul to damnation and still hold that God is love.

What Paul says—and we must say too—is this: if God wills to save you who are a sinner, that is his pure grace. That he does so will, he tells you in Christ. If you refuse God's offer, you run the risk of perishing.

In short, Paul would have agreed with P. T. Forsyth:[1] 'We are all predestined in love to life sooner or later— *if we will.*'

[1] *This Life and the Next* (London, 1946), 16.

# 7

# THE LORD AND THE APOSTLE

WAS Paul the supreme interpreter of Jesus and his Gospel,
or was he, as some have averred, its great corrupter?

It is an old question, much discussed in these last hundred
years. In earlier chapters we have made our own answer to
it tolerably clear. But since books still appear which suggest
that Paul seriously distorted, if he did not actually pervert,
the Gospel of Jesus, we must now show, by a stated case,
that the charge is false.

I

At the beginning of this century many scholars who discussed this problem stultified their whole approach to it by
a false start. Their mistake was the simple but serious one
of comparing Jesus and Paul as religious types or personali-
ties. When they started by asking, Had Jesus and Paul the
same religion? they posed the wrong question and inevitably
got the wrong answer.

It was (let us remember) the hey-day of Liberal Protestantism when the religion of Jesus could be summed up as
the paternalistic theism of the Sermon on the Mount and the
Lord's Prayer, and the great Liberal scholar Harnack[1] could
declare that 'the Gospel, as Jesus proclaimed it, had to do
with the Father only, and not with the Son'. Accordingly,
when men compared the religion of Paul with the religion of

[1] *What is Christianity?* 144.

Jesus, they naturally concluded that Paul had substituted a complicated religion about Jesus for an originally simple Gospel of Jesus. By putting the person of Jesus at the centre of his religion and investing him with the trappings of dogma and mysticism Paul had transformed the Galilean Gospel into a cosmic drama of redemption. So they came to talk of Paul as 'the second founder of Christianity'.[1]

These men made two fundamental mistakes. First, they ignored, or denied, the Messianic aspects of Christ's person and work. Second, they sought to compare two really incomparable things—the Jesus of the Gospels in *his* historical situation and the apostle's Christ in *his*.

In fact, if we are to proceed scientifically, Jesus and Paul ought to be confronted not as religious types but *in their historical relation to each other*.[2]

Let us put it this way. Only if Paul had been a disciple of Jesus, trained in his school and primarily concerned to transmit and interpret his teaching to others, would it be logically legitimate to compare the religion of Jesus with the theology of Paul. But Paul was not such a disciple; in fact Jesus never had such a disciple. Paul was an apostle who proclaimed the death and resurrection of Jesus as a great saving act of God. In their handling of this problem the Liberals made a methodological error. The only relevant and proper question here is: *Did Paul's Gospel faithfully fulfil the intention of Jesus as we know it from the Gospels, or did he falsify it by abandoning all that Jesus lived and died for?*

Before we answer this question, let us remember that between Jesus and Paul stood the *Urgemeinde*—the earliest Church. Now it is one notable achievement of modern scholarship that it has shown that, however much Paul put

[1] Wrede in his *Paulus* (1907), 103.
[2] A. Fridrichsen, *The Root of the Vine* (London, 1953), 38.

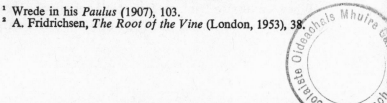

his own stamp on it, in the essentials of their Gospel Paul and the first Christians were at one. Thus is confirmed a claim that Paul himself made nineteen hundred years ago—*vide* I Cor. 15.3-11, 'But what matter I or they (Peter, James and the rest)? This is what we all proclaim, and this is what you believed.' Our question therefore is: Did the earliest Christians—and Paul after them—fulfil or falsify the Gospel of Jesus?

It is not too much to say that in our day, thanks to the rediscovery and better understanding of the eschatology of the Gospels, we now know, as the Liberals did not, what Jesus' Gospel really was. It was a message of 'realized' or, better, 'inaugurated' eschatology. Jesus began his Galilean ministry with the proclamation that the Reign of God had dawned—God had begun to take to himself his great power and reign. That Reign was being realized in himself and his ministry. Calling himself the Son of Man, Jesus believed his destiny to be that of the Servant Messiah, the One who should bring God's Kingdom to men by his representative suffering and death as the Servant of the Lord. His whole ministry he conceived as a great campaign of the Kingdom of God against the kingdom of evil; and he saw it as moving inexorably to a supreme crisis in the dealings of God with men, a crisis which would involve not only his atoning death 'for many' but also his triumph over death, a crisis which would bring God's Reign 'in power' and, with it, judgment on old Israel and the rise of a new People of God. Finally, he seems to have seen that crisis against the background of a great final consummation when God would complete his saving purpose in grace and judgment. In that faith, that conviction, Jesus went to the Cross, and, as the Gospels go on to tell, to his triumph.

When we turn to Paul, we find that he too looks forward to a final consummation which he calls the Parousia. But just as surely he looks back to the Cross and Resurrection of Jesus as a great completed act of God through which believers in the risen Lord may gain forgiveness and new life, be numbered among God's People (which he calls 'Christ's Body') and receive the power and guidance of the Holy Spirit.

Thus Paul's theology (and with it the *kerygma* of the first Christians) is, as Kümmel[1] puts it, 'faith's answer' to the saving work of God which Jesus proclaimed, embodied and accomplished; and between Jesus and Paul there emerges a deep, fundamental continuity. Yet if there is continuity, there is also one capital difference between them. Jesus, as the Gospels show, goes to the Cross as *Viator*,[2] as the pilgrim Son of God who travels by faith the road appointed by his Father. *Per contra*, Paul, as the herald of the risen Lord, looks back on the finished journey and all the blessings it brings with it. In other words, the discrepancy between Jesus and Paul is simply the difference of situations before and after Easter and Pentecost. What differentiates Paul and the first Christians from Jesus is that for them the New Age has come in power with the death, resurrection and exaltation of Jesus. With these events the period of the Law is over (cf. Luke 16.16 with Rom. 10.4); the righteousness of God has become a *fait accompli*; the new *Ecclesia* of God is a reality; the Holy Spirit has come; and Christians are 'in Christ' sons of God, enjoying even now a foretaste of the perfected salvation of God.

The point about continuity can be made in another way—by showing that the Church's earliest Gospel, which formed the basis of Paul's, was in fact rooted in the Gospel which Jesus preached.

[1] W. G. Kümmel, *Heilsgeschehen und Heilsgeschichte*, 456.
[2] As one who presses forward to the goal, not as one who has reached it (*comprehensor*).

Here, in outline, is the earliest kerygma as reconstructed by modern scholarship:

The prophecies are fulfilled, and the New Age has begun.
The Messiah, born of David's line, has appeared.
He is Jesus of Nazareth, God's Servant, who
Went about doing good and healing by God's power,
Was crucified according to God's purpose,
Was raised from the dead on the third day,
Is now exalted to God's right hand,
And will come in glory for judgment.
Therefore let all repent, believe, and be baptized for
the forgiveness of sins and the gift of the Holy Spirit.

Now go back to the gospels:

The claim that the prophecies were fulfilled corresponds to the claim with which Jesus opened his Galilean ministry, 'The (appointed) time has fully come' (Mark 1.15).

Jesus is the Messiah, said the first preachers. Our Lord knew himself to be the Messiah (Luke 7.18-23; Mark 14.61f.), even if during his ministry he veiled his claim. Likewise he interpreted his Messiahship in terms of Isaiah's Servant of the Lord (Mark 8.31, 9.31, 10.45, 14.21; Luke 22.37).

As the *kerygma* attributes Jesus' 'mighty works' to the fact that 'God was with him' (Acts 10.38), so Jesus declared his miracles to be wrought by the power of God (Luke 11.20; cf. John 14.10).

'Christ's death accorded with God's purpose in the scriptures,' said the apostles (I Cor. 15.3). Jesus predicted his atoning death in words that echo Isa. 53 (Mark 10.45, 14.24).

'Raised from the dead on the third day according to the scriptures,' declared the apostles (I Cor. 15.4). Jesus forecast his triumph over death in words which probably echo Hos. 6.2.[1]

[1] F. C. Burkitt, *JTS*. ii., 102f.; G. Delling, *TWNT*. II, 592; G. B. Caird, *St Luke* (London, 1963), 130.

'Exalted to God's right hand,' was the apostolic testimony. 'You will see the Son of Man sitting at the right hand of power' said Jesus before Caiaphas (Mark 14.62).

'Repent, be baptized and receive the Holy Spirit,' ran the apostles' summons. Jesus promised his followers the power and guidance of the Spirit (Mark 13.11; Luke 12.12; Matt. 10.10, etc.).

The other point about continuity-cum-difference between Jesus and Paul can be briefly amplified:

The apostles' *kerygma* was essentially threefold: (1) The prophecies are fulfilled; (2) the New Age has come with the coming of Christ; (3) Therefore repent and believe.

Jesus' proclamation had also three parts: (1) The prophecies are fulfilled; (2) the Reign of God has dawned; (3) therefore repent and believe.

In both *kerygmas*, items (1) and (3) are the same. But if we examine item (2), we find that the proclamation of the ministry, death and resurrection of Jesus has replaced the proclamation of the dawning of the Kingdom of God. And if we ask what has made the difference, the answer is: the events of Easter and Pentecost. The Gospel of Christ, which was the Gospel of Paul and the earliest Christians, has replaced the Gospel of the Kingdom, because by his death and resurrection Christ became the Kingdom, became all that the Kingdom contained. As Forsyth put it[1]

The Gospel of the Kingdom was Christ in essence; Christ was the Gospel of the Kingdom in power. The Kingdom was Christ in a mystery; Christ was the publication, the establishment of the Kingdom. He was the truth of his own greatest Gospel. It is wherever He is. To have Him is to ensure it.

We conclude that the Gospel of the earliest Christians— and of Paul after them—is, if we allow for the difference

[1] *The Person and Place of Jesus Christ*, 132.

made by the first Easter Day and Pentecost, the fulfilment, not the distortion, of the Gospel which Jesus preached. Jesus and Paul are not at variance; they are at one.

II

In the second half of this chapter we propose to show that in their views of man's situation before God, the Lord and his apostle are in agreement.

*Prima facie*, the very suggestion of agreement here may seem absurd. On what may be called 'our human predicament' men have often assumed a wide cleavage between Jesus and Paul. They have contrasted the simple and glad 'religion of Jesus' with the gloomy theology of the apostle. They have supposed that Jesus held fairly optimistic views of man and his 'salvability' in contrast with Paul's sombre doctrines of man's guilt and God's wrath. They have said, blandly and anachronistically, 'Jesus was a Pelagian; Paul an Augustinian.'

(*a*) To show the falseness of this antithesis, let us begin by noting that *in their attitude to the Law* Jesus and Paul essentially agree.

For both, *the Law is the revelation of God's will.* Time and time again Jesus assumes its validity and truth. When he is asked, 'What must I do to inherit eternal life?' he answers, 'You know the commandments: Do not kill, do not commit adultery, etc.' (Mark 10.17ff.). Challenged to name the chief commandment, he points to Deut. 6.4f. and Lev. 19.18 (Mark 12.29ff.). And he declares that he came not to abolish the law and the prophets but to fulfil them (Matt. 5.17).

Likewise Paul holds the Law to be the revelation of God's

will for men. Although he says that since the coming of faith the Law as a system of salvation is finished (Gal. 3.23ff.), he declares that the Law is 'holy' and 'spiritual' and the commandment 'holy and just and good' (Rom. 7.12-14). And he agrees that he who fulfils the Law gains life (Rom. 2.10, 10.5).

Observe next that both Jesus and Paul lay the emphasis on the *moral* demands of the law. It is to these 'Do not kill, etc.' that Jesus directs the Rich Young Ruler (Mark 10. 17ff.). In Mark 7 he plays off the Fifth Commandment against the Scribes and Pharisees who practise Corban. And he singles out 'justice, mercy and good faith' as 'the weightier matters of the Law' (Matt. 23.23). Paul does the same When, discussing the Law in Rom. 7.7, he has to choose a concrete example, he chooses the Tenth Commandment, the only Commandment that deals with inward impulse rather than overt act. No less significantly in Rom. 2.14f. he regards the Gentiles' 'conscience'—the moral law within—as their equivalent for the Jewish Law.

Finally, both Jesus and Paul take *the commandment of love to be the core and kernel of the Law*. Cf. Mark 12.29-31 with Rom. 13.8-10. 'Love is the fulfilling of the law.'

But does not Paul say that the Law drives man to sin, and declare that God's grace alone, and not works of law, can save men (Gal. 2.16)? He does indeed; yet he does not say that works of law are not God's will—quite the contrary! What Paul means is that every attempt to *earn* salvation by works is not only foredoomed to failure but is presumptuous sin against God (Rom. 10.3f.).

Jesus, who draws his images and pictures from daily life, does not of course theologize about sin as Paul does. Yet if his language differs, his view is the same. The servant who has 'done the things commanded' has 'no cause for boasting'. So we also (says Jesus in his parable, Luke 17.7-10), when we have done all our duty, must own ourselves 'unworthy servants', since God's commandment is incomparably more radical than man's. 'Is it enough to forgive an offending brother seven times?' Peter asks his Master hopefully. 'Seven times?' replies Jesus in effect. 'No, seventy times seven!' There is no 'enough' with God (Matt. 18.21f.). And Jesus no less than Paul knows that for the legalist in religion God's sheer grace to undeserving men must ever remain a stumbling-block (Matt. 20.1-15).

(b) But we can carry the parallel between Jesus' teaching and Paul's yet further.

Consider next the doctrine of *justification by faith*. If anything has the right to be called Paul's own special Christian doctrine, surely it is this. If a man would 'get right with God', Paul teaches in Galatians and Romans, he must forever renounce the attempt to establish his own righteousness before God and, owning his utter unworthiness, cast himself upon God's forgiving grace in Christ. Surely on a theological issue like this there is a great gulf between the Lord and his apostle!

There is not: on the theological principle the Lord and the apostle are at one. Take first the greatest of Christ's parables (Luke 15.11-32). Without a word of forensic language, it teaches exactly what Paul means by justification; and its message can be summed up in a phrase of Paul's, 'God who justifies the ungodly' (Rom. 4.5). If we ask first, What does the parable teach about God? the answer is, God is a God of sheer grace—the God who freely forgives the man who has no claim on his forgiveness, who can only say 'I have sinned against heaven and before you; I am no longer worthy to be called your son.' If next we ask, What does the parable teach about man's salvation; the answer is, Not by works (this was the Elder Brother's plea) but by a heart-felt confession of his own unworthiness and a casting of himself on God's mercy, is man saved. As Sanday and Headlam say[1]

Reduced to its simplest elements, justification is simply free forgiveness. The parable of the Prodigal Son is a picture of it. . . . At bottom the teaching of the Gospels is not really different from Paul's. Only one is tenderly and pathetically human, where the other is a system of Jewish scholasticism.

Pursuing our parallel further, let us compare the Beatitudes of Jesus (which are congratulatory, not hortatory) with a passage from Paul like I Cor. 1.26-31. Jesus pronounces God's blessing on 'the poor', 'the mourners', 'the humble', and the men who 'hunger and thirst to see right prevail'—in a word, on all the lowly and despised of this world who, knowing their own insufficiency, are content to rest all their hope on the mercy of God. Do not these 'makarisms' of Jesus find a true spiritual echo and fulfilment in what Paul says to the 'saints' of Corinth: 'Think', Paul says, 'what sort of people you are, whom God has called: not many wise, by worldly standards, not many powerful, not many of noble birth. But God chose what is low and despised in this world, even things that are not, to bring to nothing things that are, so that no human being might boast in the presence of God.'

Look finally at the parable of the Pharisee and the Publican (Luke 18.9-14). Not the Pharisee who parades his own religious achievements before God, who 'boasts' (as Paul would say) of his 'works', but the Tax-collector who cries out of a deep sense of his own unworthiness, 'God be merciful to me, a sinner,' is justified (*dedikaiōmenos*) in God's sight. This is not merely Paul's doctrine; it is his very word. Rightly does Jeremias[2] say that the apostle's doctrine of justification goes back to Jesus:

[1] *Romans*, 36f.
[2] *The Central Message of the New Testament* (London, 1965), 69f.

The doctrine (Paul's) is nothing else but Jesus' message of the God who wants to deal with sinners, expressed in theological terms. Jesus says: I came not to call the righteous but sinners; Paul says, The ungodly man is justified. Jesus says, Blessed are the poor; Paul says, We are justified by grace. Jesus says: Let the dead bury their dead (a powerful word which implies that outside the Kingdom one finds nothing but death); Paul says, He who is justified by faith will have life. The vocabulary is different, but the content is the same.

(c) There is one more argument to be thrown into the scale of proof. Paradoxical as it may sound, it is true to say that *the Sermon on the Mount and the Epistle to the Romans belong together—concur in their conviction that we are united in our status as sinners before God.*

This is a hard saying, if we stick to the concordance and study words only. In Romans Paul has much to say about sin (as a personified force, with a capital S); Jesus, if we count only specific words for sin, little or nothing in his Sermon on the Mount. But to conclude from this that Jesus, by contrast with Paul, is less seriously concerned about the gravity of sin, would be a grave error.

In any attempt to appraise our Lord's attitude to sin, we can begin by listing the actual sins which he condemned— pride, hypocrisy, ingratitude, lack of compassion, the unforgiving temper. Or we can pick out sayings like 'If you then being evil . . .' where Jesus quietly assumes 'the corruption of man's heart'. Or we can dwell on his terrible warnings against causing 'little ones' to stumble (Matt. 18.6f.; Luke 17.1f.). Nevertheless, we shall never understand how seriously he accounted sin till we see that his view of sin is *an inference from his view of righteousness*. It is here that the Sermon supplies our best evidence, especially the six great antitheses of Matt. 5.21-48, in which Jesus sets forth the contrast between the Law of Moses as a code of commandments to be carried out, and God's true will for men. As of old Isaiah 'saw the Lord high and lifted up' and in a blinding flash realized his own sinfulness, so we may suppose the men on whose ears and hearts first fell the revelation of God's holy will in the Sermon, saw the Divine ideal and knew how far they fell short of it. From time to time one hears people saying that they 'like' the Sermon on the Mount. It is in fact the most damning indictment of human nature in all literature. 'There is no account of sin', says Ryder Smith,[1] 'to match the Sermon'. Who is sufficient to meet these merciless demands? Who is able to fulfil them? If that is the Divine ideal—if that is how God means his children to live—we may well say with the Publican, 'God have mercy on us all, sinners.'

In the teaching of Jesus, then, 'no one is good' by God's standards. All 'come short of the glory of God' as it confronts them in the radical demands of the Sermon. Anger, lustful desire, hatred, vengefulness, all are transgressions of God's will. If we succumb to them, as we do, there is nothing left but to acknowledge with Paul

> All have swerved aside,
> All have gone bad,
> There is none who does good, no, not one (Rom. 3.12).

Let us sum up. Jesus does not use the vocabulary or the thought-forms of his apostle, as he does not speculate about sin's origin or psychologize about its workings. But in their conviction that we are united in our status as sinners before God and that God's grace avails not for the self-righteous but for penitent sinners, the Lord and the Apostle are again at one.

[1] *The Bible Doctrine of Salvation* (London, 1946), 170.

### III

If there is any cogency in the arguments of this chapter, two things have been established. First, it is false to say that Paul preached a different religion or revelation from Jesus. It is the same *Heilstat Gottes*—the same saving act of God—which is the central theme of both the Gospels and the Epistles. But whereas Jesus, who not only announces but embodies this *Heilstat*, speaks of it as *Viator* (rather than *Comprehensor*) on this side of Calvary, Paul speaks of it from the vantage-point of Easter and Pentecost, that is, proclaims its effectuation 'in power' by the Resurrection and the coming of the Spirit. Second, it is false to say that in their views of sin and salvation Jesus and Paul are at variance or conflict: different as their words, images, and concepts are, they are, *au fond*, in agreement. Yet there is one quite decisive and ultimate difference between Jesus and Paul, and none realized it more clearly than Paul himself. It is this: Jesus knows himself to be the Christ of God, the Bringer to men of God's final salvation; Paul is but the servant and envoy of this Christ. In short, the difference between Jesus and Paul is the difference suggested by the title of this chapter. Paul is the apostle; Jesus is the Lord.

# 8

## PAUL FOR TODAY

I T is now 1900 years since Paul 'taught righteousness to the
world . . . and was taken up into the Holy Place'.[1] Not
only so, but we know that not long after his death his Christianity suffered eclipse so that, as Harnack said, only one
man in the second century—Marcion—understood Paul,
and he misunderstood him!

Yet Paul's Christianity did not die. On the contrary, it
became in succeeding centuries 'incomparably the greatest
source of spiritual revivals in the Christian Church'.[2] How
stands the matter now? Is Paul for us just 'an old fogey out
of the Bible', or being dead, does he yet speak to us, so that,
as Karl Barth[3] puts it, 'if we are enlightened by the bright-
ness of his answers, these answers must be ours too'?

Before we essay an answer, let us briefly recall what
Christianity according to St Paul really was.

Men, made for fellowship with God, are separated from
him by sin. Of our own strength we cannot save ourselves—
cannot break the deadly grip that indwelling sin lays on us.
We are guilty men at the bar of God, and no works of ours
can avail to put us right with him.

But (says Paul) it has pleased God of his grace to bridge
the chasm between his holiness and our sin. In the Gospel
of Christ God offers us his forgiveness, a forgiveness
grounded in the Cross. As we respond to it by faith, which

[1] Clement of Rome.
[2] Denney, *The Christian Doctrine of Reconciliation*, 179.
[3] *The Epistle to the Romans*, i.

is the soul's obedient Yes to God's offer, God reinstates us
in his favour, and this is the first step on the road to spiritual
safety.

Thus reconciled to God, we are potentially new men
living a new life. This new life is, first, a community life,
because by baptism we are incorporated in the new People
of God, of which Christ is the living Head. Next, it is a life
empowered by the Holy Spirit. And, finally, it is a life lived
'according to Christ', i.e., after his pattern and example.

Yet this new life is but the earnest of that perfected salvation to be ours at the End when Christ will come in glory,
the resurrection and last judgment will take place, and those
who are Christ's will gain the heavenly life God has prepared for them that love him.

Can we make the substance of that Faith our own today?
This is the issue now to be discussed.

In a new and suggestive exegesis of II Cor. 2.14-17, T. W.
Manson[1] makes Paul speak of the revelation of God in
Christ as God's 'life-giving remedy against sin', in a way
which reminds us of the old evangelical jingle

> Life is short,
> Death is sure,
> Sin is the wound,
> Christ is the cure.

Before we consider 'the cure', we must see whether Paul's
diagnosis of 'the wound' is accurate and convincing.

When Browning wrote— ,

> Tis the Faith that launched point blank her dart
> At the head of a life—taught Original Sin,
> The corruption of man's heart,

he was aligning himself with a long succession of Christian
thinkers going back to Paul. Down nineteen centuries the

[1] *Studia Paulina*, 155-162.

Church's teaching—with occasional protests from men like Pelagius who have asserted that man *need* not sin—has been founded on what Paul said about man's condition before God. 'Original sin, the corruption of man's heart' was the major premise from which Paul started. He held a doctrine of general, though not total, human depravity. Sin was a state, not simply an incident without antecedents and consequences. More, it was a universal state, something which affects every son of Adam: like runners in the strawberry bed, we are all connected up through a common life-root, and through that root-system flows evil. The 'power of sin' for Paul was the Law, by which he meant not only that God's law shows up sin for what it is, but also that it actually provokes to sin and so brings us under God's displeasure. For this sin we men are accountable by God, and yet by no *tour de force* of human effort can we save ourselves from it and put ourselves right with God. For 'the unrighteousness of men' only 'the righteousness of God' revealed in Christ will avail.

Such is Paul's picture of our human predicament. It is a sombre one. But is it true? Is not modern man justified in dismissing it as 'the delusion of the synagogue' or the morbid vapourings of a first-century pathological introvert? Some grain of truth we may find in it—we know, for example, that the revolt against a law which imposes itself on our nature is something not merely Jewish but human and universal. Yet the doubt asserts itself that Paul's doctrine is hopelessly outmoded and is bound up with belief in the 'Fall' of a historical first man named Adam. After all, Paul was a man of his time; he knew nothing of the scientific doctrine of heredity; he had never heard of Darwin or Freud. How can modern man, who values his intellectual integrity, take Paul's account of our spiritual predicament as true?

Let us preface our reply by observing that, in order to maintain that his diagnosis is true, it is not necessary to accept every part of Paul's account of sin. Thus we are not bound to believe with Paul that the sinfulness of all men stems from Adam's act of disobedience. On the contrary, where the origin of sin is concerned, we may be content to say, 'We do not know how or when it originated; we only know that it is here.' But the main question is this: Is Paul's picture of man as sinner still substantially true? Or must we consent with some that what Paul calls sin is basically ignorance, to be cured by education, or acquisitiveness, to be cured by the abolition of private property, or good in disguise—the soul's growing pains—to be remedied by wise doses of 'sweetness and light'?

Paul no doubt held man to be inherently and incorrigibly sinful. But nineteen centuries have passed, and in that time what progress man has made! How enlightened we have become! If we could affirm that evil was due simply to external causes, or was a mere 'hang-over' from our animal ancestry destined to pass away as the evolutionary process bore man onward and upward; or that higher education and improved psychological techniques would deliver man from his ignorance, dispel his guilt complexes and, in short, turn bad men into good ones, then we might dispense with St Paul as we dispense with the doctor when the patient is obviously well set on the high road to good health. But the question is, Does an honest look at mankind today warrant such a confidence?

Today we are much more disposed to listen to St Paul than we were, say, sixty years ago. Then the belief in progress was at its zenith: man's onward and upward march seemed sure, limitless and irreversible. The mood of the time seemed to wipe out the black miseries of previous centuries. Man, it was thought, 'was out of the woods at last'.

All this talk about sin was merely the stock-in-trade of a morbid and outdated theology. So it was not surprising that even Christian people, catching the *Zeitgeist*, decided that Paul was 'a back number' and put their trust in 'a God without wrath who brings men without sin into a kingdom without judgment through the ministrations of a Christ without a Cross'.[1] 'God is not mocked,' says Paul: but the men of that day little guessed how soon the wrath of God was to be revealed against the unrighteousness of men.

How stands the matter now? By the two colossal disasters of our time and their awful aftermaths we have learned, in blood and tears, how dread a laboratory of good and evil is the heart of man, and how apparently great and cultured nations can deliver themselves over to insensate cruelty, madness and sin. The notion that evil is something superficial and external, clinging to man's heart as the barnacles to the ship's hull, is exploded. Discredited, too, is religious moralism's idea of sin as something merely incidental, a wrong choice, a not-now. And even some of our philosophers and politicians are beginning to consent that there is much to be said for the Christian dogma of Original Sin.[2]

The evils, then, of which Paul writes are not strange to us, though Paul's way of talking about them may often be. It follows, therefore, that if we are to present Paul's Gospel to the men of today, we must begin with the fact of a fallen world and the reality of sin. But precisely there lies one of

[1] H. R. Niebuhr, *The Kingdom of God in America* (New York), 193.
[2] The late C. E. M. Joad told us in his *Recovery of Belief* how as a young man having unquestioningly accepted Herbert Spencer's doctrine of evolutionary optimism, he was driven by the bitter logic of events to avow that the Christian account of evil and sin was a pretty accurate appraisal of the human situation. Recently Mr R. H. S. Crossman is reported as saying: 'To judge by the facts, there is a great deal more to be said for the Christian doctrine of Original Sin than for Rousseau's theory of the noble savage or Marx's of the classless society.'

our difficulties. Brunner[1] has said that the doctrine of Original Sin is one of the things in the Christian Faith which are
'scandals' to modern man. The 'scandal' has really nothing
to do with Gen. 3 and the attempt to take it as literal history.
Unless we are invincible 'fundamentalists', we know that
Adam is Hebrew for a human being, or mankind collec-
tively, and that Gen. 3 is to be regarded as 'a true myth',
that, though Eden is on no map and Adam's fall fits no
historical calendar, that chapter witnesses to a dimension of
human experience as real now as at the beginning of man's
story—in plain terms, we are fallen creatures and the tale of
Adam and Eve is the story of you and me.

No, sin is a religious concept, it is crime and rebellion
against God; and the trouble is that modern man does not
recognize it in himself or others as such because he has lost
that awareness of the living and holy God which makes it
sin. So he tends to dodge the responsibility for it. He may
lay the blame on corrupting institutions (which he believes
he can remake) or on the confusions of ignorance (which
higher education will cure) or on psychological maladjust-
ments (which better psychology will eliminate), not discern-
ing that they are but symptoms of that deeper disease which
Paul called indwelling sin, the corruption of man's heart.

More than that, confronted and depressed by the omni-
presence of evil, he is prone to turn nihilist and write the
world off as a meaningless chaos.

If then, with Paul, we are to face men with the fact of sin,
our aim should not be to deepen despair but to kindle hope.
We have to teach men that the world is not a nihilist's night-
mare but God's world into which alien and chaotic things
have entered. We have to proclaim both God and his forgiveness—God, in order that men may see the nature of their
sin as rebellion against his holy love; and forgiveness, that

[1] *The Scandal of Christianity* (London, 1951), Ch. 3.

they may consciously accept responsibility for actual sin committed. Men today know only too well that the world is mysteriously and radically wrong. To enable them to see the true nature of their darkness, we must show them the light— Paul's light—the light of the Gospel of the grace of God who was in Christ reconciling the world to himself.

II

For the sin of man, Paul declares, the only cure is the grace of God in Christ. We cannot save ourselves by our 'works'; but what we cannot do, God has done for us in Christ crucified—

'All are justified by God's free grace, through his act of liberation in the person of Christ Jesus.'

'Christ died for us while we were yet sinners, and that is God's own proof of his love towards us.'

'God was in Christ reconciling the world to himself.'[1]

There at the Cross, in very deed, sinful man gets the proof of a love of God that expiates his sin and liberates him from its bondage for new life. This new start and status, this gift, free and undeserved, of a new possibility of life, Paul calls 'redemption', 'justification' and 'reconciliation'. God, taking the gracious initiative, offers it to us in Christ: and as we accept it in faith, God delivers us, pardons us, and sets us right with himself. The first and decisive step on the road to salvation has been taken.

The question is, Are these only the moribund catchwords of an antiquated soteriology, or do they stand for something which we ourselves can experience today?

Let us consider some of the doubts and difficulties which Paul's doctrine raises for modern man.

[1] Rom. 3.24, 5.8; II Cor. 5.19 (NEB).

Some there are who fear that the reconciling power which streamed from Christ in the first century may have faded and failed with the passing of the centuries. They feel that the experience of which Paul writes is tied to the historical Christ who stands at a far and ever-widening distance from us. This is because they forget the Holy Spirit whose role it is to 'take of the things of Christ and show them unto us'. The Christ of the first century—the Christ who called Peter in Galilee and 'arrested' Paul on the Damascus Road—does not belong only to the past. He is our eternal Contemporary. The Spirit makes him such, and it is not from Palestine, or from the first century, but here and now he is to be known and his reconciling power experienced.

Others there are who feel that the religious experience implied by words like 'justification' and 'reconciliation' can mean very little to themselves today. Most of us Christians (they say) have not passed over from Judaism (as Paul did) or from heathenism (as many of his converts did) to Christianity. On the contrary, brought up in conventional Christian homes, and familiar with Christian teaching and practice from earliest days, we have no need for the kind of deliverance or conversion Paul describes. To others who have lived godless lives or have 'lapsed from grace', Paul's message may well come as a 'power of God unto salvation'. But, for ourselves, Paul's Gospel here does not 'ring a bell' in our Christian experience—has little reality for us.

If this objection is sound, must not Paul's doctrine of salvation be irrelevant for many?

Let us grant, to begin with, that men find their way into God's Kingdom by various ways, and that the experience of a man converted from plain godlessness may well appear quite other from that of one brought up, as the saying goes, 'in the bosom of the Church'. But are the two kinds of Christian experience so basically opposed to each other, as the objection suggests? Is it not true that no man, whatever his previous faith or folly, can save himself? Is it not true that we all are utterly dependent on the grace of God?

Consider, again, the fact that (as Denney said) down nineteen centuries Paul's Gospel has been the greatest source of religious revival within the Christian Church. This fact certainly does not suggest that the bulk of people in Christendom, past or present, have found its message alien, irrelevant, unreal.

But, to carry our answer one stage further, is this the true antithesis we have been considering, the antithesis between those who have entered the Kingdom one way and those who have entered it by another? Is the true antithesis not rather between those who have really committed themselves to God through Christ, and those who have not? And if a man tells us that he finds Paul's doctrine of salvation unreal and that his 'word of the Cross' wakes no answering echo in his heart and conscience, might he not well ask himself if he has ever really made the venture of Christian faith and, in Forsyth's phrase, 'committed his whole soul and future to Christ for God and eternity'?

Finally, there are others who feel that the whole issue of faith and works, which seems to bulk so large in Paul's thinking, is now something as dead as the dodo.

Let us admit that Paul's language has an old-fashioned ring about it, but let us not for one moment suppose that men no longer rely on 'works'. The people who think they can save themselves are still with us, both outside the Church and in it.

Everywhere men seek, as of old, to satisfy their conscience by the performance of duty, or by telling themselves that they have done their duty, or that, at least, they are as good as those who

D

make a profession of religion, and better, perhaps, for they are not hypocrites.[1]

'Both Jesus and Paul agree,' Professor Jeremias[2] has written, 'that no man is so far from God as the self-righteous person.' True then, it is still true. We still number among our congregations hundreds and hundreds of people who hear the Gospel of God's forgiving grace in Christ without understanding, because they have persuaded themselves they have no need to repent, no need to be pardoned. Only when they learn how insufficient is all their boasted goodness, only when they become so dissatisfied not with this or that fault in their lives but with their whole character, that they are ready to cry with Christ's publican, 'God be merciful to me a sinner', will they begin to realize that Paul's Gospel speaks to their condition and offers them the remedy they need.

Not to 'the wise and the prudent'—to sophisticated modern men confident that they can save themselves by one technique or another—but to the 'babes'—to the men who know what despair of themselves means and are marked by a great simplicity—does God reveal the secret of his grace in Christ. This was the teaching of the Lord and of his apostle. It has not ceased to be true.

In short, to say that the deliverance of which Paul writes is alien, remote and unintelligible is to fly in the face of centuries of Christian experience. What the Kingswood colliers testified in the eighteenth century—

> He breaks the power of cancelled sin,
> He sets the prisoners free

has been found true by thousands upon thousands from Augustine to Bunyan, from William Cowper to Thomas

---

[1] Campbell Moody, *The Purpose of Jesus*, 142.
[2] *ET* Sept. 1955, 369.

Chalmers, from James Denney to Billy Graham. Whatever in Paul is outmoded and antiquated, this article in his Christianity is not.

The real problem before us today is that of communicating Paul's Gospel in terms that will come home to modern man. Paul had his own set of idioms, thought-forms and metaphors for describing how God in Christ had wrought rescue for sinful man. Can we still use them today and hope that they will be meaningful in a world so utterly different in many ways from Paul's?

If we are honest, I think we must admit that the grand old word 'redemption' has lost much of its force. In Paul's day the metaphor of 'redeeming' and the custom of 'sacral manumission' were matter of familiar experience and knowledge to all his hearers. Nowadays 'redemption' suggests only the pawnshop. What of Paul's law-court metaphor 'justification'? In the tradition of the Reformed Churches, it has of course had a long and honoured history. Yet who will claim that, without long and learned explanations, it can now be meaningfully and effectively employed?

On the other hand, if it is true, as our scholars tell us, that 'justification is just forgiveness—sheer forgiveness', then it is legitimate to dispense, in preaching, with forensic terms and to put Paul's truth in quite personal and human ways.

This brings us to his third term 'reconciliation', which, for modern men, is surely the best of all three. To begin with, it states the whole problem in the language of personal relations, a language which never grows out of date; and, second, it answers to a fundamental human need; for reconciliation to reality, however that reality be conceived, is something, as the great writers from Lucretius and Virgil to Goethe and Wordsworth testify, elemental and universal, a hunger of the soul which all men know and feel.

Our suggestion, then, is that the language of the home may move the men of our day when the language of the slave-market or of the law-court leaves them cold. And have we not the best of all warrants for using it? May not the greatest of our Lord's parables serve as guide and exemplar? What is the doctrine of the parable of the Prodigal Son if it is not the doctrine of the God who justifies the ungodly, who acquits guilty men—a doctrine couched not in scholastic but in tenderly human terms? The heart of the matter is that men today are still in the plight of the Prodigal—alienated by their sin and guilt from the All-Father. This is the first thing they must learn, and they can only learn it through a despair like the Prodigal's. But such despair is the proper soil for the good seed of the Gospel of God's grace in Christ. Then they must hear 'the old, old story' proclaimed with all the vivid relevance we can command—that the Father has given his only Son to deal finally with their sin, and that what is needed is repentance and the decision of faith.

### III

When a sinful man has been reconciled to God through Christ, he enters on 'newness of life', is potentially a new man living in a new world, even if bits of 'the old man' still cling to him, like bits of eggshell to the young chick, and because, being still 'in the flesh', he is still exposed to the downward pulls and pressures of his 'lower nature'. But the power of his old master, Sin, is broken, he has acquired a new master, Christ, and he is summoned, with the Holy Spirit's help, to fight the good fight against all the forces of evil. So Paul describes salvation as a present experience.

Let us look more closely at this new life described by

Paul in order to see how far his teaching about it is true and tenable by us today.

Its first mark is that it is new life 'in Christ'—life in a community whose head is the living Christ. Thus it has two orientations—a vertical and a horizontal. To begin with, it is a life of fellowship with a living and reigning Lord; and, second, and springing from the first, it is a life shared with others who confess the same Lord.

There are still those among us who imagine that the Christian life is a kind of harking-back to the first century in the endeavour to follow Christ as the first disciples did in Galilee. They need to learn from Paul that the essence of being a Christian lies in fellowship with a *contemporary* Christ, a Christ no longer cramped and confined as in 'the days of his flesh' but 'let loose in the world', by the Resurrection and the coming of the Spirit, to be a ubiquitous and universal Saviour. Further, for Paul, this fellowship with Christ was not something felt by only a few people in hours of special exaltation; it was ordinary Christian experience, something to be shared by all God's People.

Should it not still be so? Phillips Brooks was once asked whether communion with Christ was necessary if one was to be a Christian. 'Communion with Christ,' he replied, 'is Christianity.' We are dealing here with something not confined to Paul and the first century but still verifiably true and real in the twentieth; with something that is, or ought to be, as the Germans say, *gemeinchristlich*; with something which resounds through all the greatest hymns of Christian experience and devotion. And it is so because we are dealing with Someone who is 'the same yesterday, today and for ever', who, having promised to be with his own 'to the end of time', joins in one communion of saints Paul and Patrick, Rutherford and Fox, David Livingstone and Charles Raven; and not these alone but countless others, unknown to fame or the history books, who have walked through the bright and dark places of this world companioned by an unseen Presence.

But it was not only a contemporary Christ that Paul preached; it was a *community* One. According to Paul, the decision of faith which commits us to Christ in the same act commits us to his Community; and the apostle would have found the greatest difficulty in comprehending a man who, claiming to be 'in Christ', i.e. a Christian, declared he 'had no use for the Church'.

Here is a Christian truth some of us Protestants have been re-discovering in the last few decades. The nineteenth century was the hey-day of religious individualism when even pious Christians might be heard saying, 'Give us more Christianity and less Church-ianity.' The Bible might 'know nothing of solitary religion', as the New Testament knows nothing of 'unattached Christians'. But some of our fathers, by failing to grasp the centrality of the Church in the New Testament, lent serious colour to the notion that the Church was an optional addendum to the soul's communion with God.

Nowadays we are realizing anew what Paul never doubted, that, though we become related to Christ singly, we cannot live in him solitarily, and that in fact all true Christian experience is ecclesiastical experience. The Church is of the *esse* of Christianity.

The other issue of importance today on which Paul can still speak to us is that of Church unity. 'There is one Body,' says the apostle; and for him the one-ness of the Church is as axiomatic as the uniqueness of the Church's Lord. It is with sheer horror that he hears of the 'parties' in Corinth: 'Is Christ divided?' And we cannot doubt that, if Paul were among us today, he would condemn our ecclesiastical divisions as roundly as he condemned the cliques in Corinth.

Happily, at long last, a welcome 'wind of change' is blowing now in all our denominations. Christians are realizing that they can no longer burke the whole issue on the plea, 'Why worry about re-union? We Christians are already one in spirit.' God is manifestly calling us Christians in this day to recover the lost unity of the Church; and all who confess the name of Christ are being summoned, by ecumenical dialogue and by co-operation with our brethren in other denominations, to work and think and pray for the healing of the broken Body of Christ.

The second mark of the new life is that it is life empowered by the Holy Spirit.

In only one letter—the brief note to Philemon—does the Holy Spirit fail to appear; for the rest, it is a case of *Circumspice*. For Paul the Christian era is 'the dispensation of the Spirit'. At baptism the convert receives the Spirit; Christian behaviour is a 'walking by the Spirit'; Christian skills are the Spirit's grace-gifts (*charismata*) and Christian virtues the Spirit's 'harvest'; and if we hope for life as immortal as Christ's own, our hope rests on the Spirit of him who raised Christ from the dead. In short, Paul sets the whole Christian life, beginning, middle and end, in the dynamic context of the Spirit.

When we read Paul's pages, so aglow with the Spirit, and then turn to the Christian scene today, do we not sometimes feel that 'there hath passed away a glory from the earth'? How dull, unexciting and void of reality seems our own church life when we contrast it with the energy and life which filled Paul's churches! Somehow the spiritual temperature has dropped; the high poetry has become flat prose; and the *Geist* has gone out of our Christian faith and hope and love.

Or, again, if we read some contemporary theology, we begin to understand why Brunner has called the Holy Spirit 'the theologians' step-child'. Bultmann and his followers, for example, have urged upon us the need for 'a new hermeneutic'[1] if the Gospel is to come home to modern men. But, alas, it is a hermeneutic without the Holy Spirit. Says Stephen Neill:

> The whole work of Bultmann can be summed up as a gallant attempt to solve the problem, to make the challenge (of the Gospel) existential without belief in the resurrection of Jesus Christ as something that actually happened, and without a doctrine of the Holy Spirit.[2]

Such a Gospel—a Gospel which does not really believe that Christ rose from the grave and which finds no place for the work of the Holy Spirit—is but a half-gospel, and 'half-gospels are like the famous mule—without pride of ancestry or hope of posterity'.[3]

Yet, if our church life so often lacks vitality and some of our theologians neglect the Holy Spirit, this does not mean that God has withdrawn his Pentecostal gift—

> The centuries go gliding,
> But still we have abiding
> With us that Spirit holy
> To make us brave and lowly.[4]

When we are tempted to suppose that the Holy Spirit no longer works in our world, it is partly because we take too limited a view, confine our view to our own corner of the vineyard and take little account of the wider world where the winds of God are blowing. So we fail to observe 'the great new fact of our time'—the existence of something

[1] See note at the end of this section.
[2] *The Interpretation of the New Testament, 1861-1961* (Oxford, 1964), 233.
[3] P. T. Forsyth.
[4] F. C. Burkitt.

like a world-wide Church following a century and a half of great missionary expansion; or the gathering momentum of the movement for re-union among Christians; or the continuing fertility of Christian thought as evidenced by the desire to recover the full dimensions of the Gospel (Karl Barth and others) and to re-state it for the men of our day (Paul Tillich and others), by the emergence of new patterns of Christian ministry to meet the needs of a quick-changing age, by the new emphasis on the apostolate of the Laity, etc., etc. Are not all these proof that the Spirit of God is moving in our world today? Nevertheless, it remains true that many of us Christians do not regard the Spirit as Paul did, i.e. not simply as the Illuminator in specifically holy things to be invoked on *ad hoc* sacred occasions, but as the Enabler of the whole Christian life. Part of the reason may be that (not unjustifiably) we suspect people who 'pretend to extraordinary manifestations of the Spirit',[1] like the Pentecostal sects proliferating in America and elsewhere. Again, bemused by a false scientific philosophy, we tend to assume that Nature is 'a closed system' impervious to any kind of supernatural invasion. And a third reason is undoubtedly just pure human sinful self-reliance—what Paul would call 'bondage to the flesh'—which is not ready to let the Spirit have his sovereign way with us.

The time has surely come for Christians to re-discover the reality of the Holy Spirit. Constant returning to Paul's great chapters on the theme—Rom. 8, II Cor. 3, Gal. 5, etc. —will help us in our quest for a fresh experience of that 'life of God in the soul of man' which inspires all true Christian thinking, willing and doing. It has been said that whatever is not apostolic is not safe. If this is true, a returning to the ancient springs of power may be the imperious Christian need of our time. 'Listen to the wind,' said

---

[1] Bishop Butler's comment on John Wesley and his followers.

our Lord to Nicodemus. 'You cannot tell where it comes from or where it goes. Yet how real and powerful a thing it is. So it is with God's Spirit. And it offers you what you need' (John 3.7f. paraphrased). Are we not, many of us, still Nicodemuses? Why should we not recover the faith that God can still work dynamically in our lives, piercing down to the deepest levels of human personality and enabling them for the tasks of Christian living?

The third mark of the new life is that it is a life lived 'according to Christ' (*kata Christon*, Col. 2.8)—according to his pattern and example.

The question therefore before us now is that of the relevance for us of Paul's Christian ethic.

It is obvious that a great many of the moral problems which vex modern Christians (The Just War, the Bomb, the Pill, etc.) never came within Paul's horizon. How, then, can he guide our Christian practice today? This is a big question, not to be adequately answered in a paragraph or two. We must, however, content ourselves with making three main points.

The first is that Paul has seized on the true secret of Gospel ethics in any age, which is that good actions are the expression of a transformed life. If (to borrow Jesus' metaphor for a moment) good fruits are to grow from it, you must first make the tree good. And the power which alone can do this—can change a human life—is the grace of God. It was this insight on which Luther fastened when he said, 'It is not good works which make a good man, but a good man who does good works.' Laws can point men to the good life; they cannot make men good. What they cannot do is to break what Paul calls 'the power of sin in the flesh', or, as we might put it today, the downward pull of our inherited racial instincts. What is needed is the implanting of a new principle of life in us which will overcome 'the old nature' and produce 'the new man after Christ'. Now the power which implants this new principle, which cleanses a man's heart and changes him, is the Gospel of God's forgiving grace in Christ; and Christian goodness, which is the response to that grace, ought to be the natural unfolding of the new life in moral action. To be sure, since we are still 'in the flesh' and exposed to the pressures of the world, ethical effort will be demanded and we shall have to hearken to Paul's 'imperatives of grace' (see Rom. 6); but this is the true spiritual theory of the matter, and as true and relevant now as then.

Our second point is that often, when Paul is handling moral issues which are now to us only of historical and antiquarian interest, he lays down principles of action which are wisely and timelessly Christian.

An obvious example from I Corinthians will serve. To eat, or not to eat, meat which had been connected with pagan sacrifices (as a lot of meat in the Corinthian butchers' shops had been), this was the problem before the Church at Corinth (I Cor. 8-10; cf. Rom. 14 where a similar issue had arisen, though here vegetarianism came into the picture). The libertarians in the Church had no scruples at all about this; the more sensitive members were, as we say, 'worried stiff' at the very idea of doing it. Though himself a stout champion of Christian freedom (see his letter to the Galatians), Paul on this issue came down firmly on the other side. 'Let not your liberty become a stumbling block to the other man' was the gist of his advice, 'or you may ruin a brother for whom Christ died'.

Except, perhaps, in some of our younger churches, this particular problem is no longer a live one with us. Today the issue is the use and abuse of alcohol (especially by those who drive cars), or the proper observance of Sunday, or the question of militancy and pacifism. But Paul's principle that love must have priority over liberty is as valid as ever. The same may be said of the other motives for Christian action which we find in his letters. One might be called Christian *Noblesse oblige*, i.e. spiritual rank imposes moral obligations on us Christians (see Phil. 1.27 and Eph. 4.1). Another might be called the *koinonia* motive, since it calls on us always to act as members of Christ's Body, and invites us, when faced with a decision, to ask ourselves, Will my proposed action build up or destroy the Body of Christ? Such principles are still valid, still capable of wide application to the problems of Christian practice today.

Thirdly, Paul's command to 'fulfil the law of Christ' and to make *agape* the master-key of Christian morals is surely as compulsive and challenging as ever.

So long as there are Christians, so long must the 'design for life' which Christ gave his followers and the example of his own life remain as a guide and challenge to the adventure of Christian living in the world. As we have seen, Paul not only quoted 'Words of the Lord' to settle every-day problems in his churches, but he wove into the fabric of his ethical exhortations the teaching of the Lord. Nowadays, Matthew's Sermon on the Mount is probably the best summary of what may be called 'the Dominical Design for the good life'. From it, however far short we come of the moral heights to which Christ calls us, we may learn how God means us to live, how to treat our neighbours, our friends, our enemies; and we are summoned, with the Holy Spirit's help, to live so far as may be according to that Dominical pattern.

The sum-total of it all is *agape*, that word in which both the Lord and his apostle found the quintessential principle of the Christian Way. But, as Paul knew, the love which in his life Jesus demanded of his disciples acquired, through his death, an even richer meaning, so that Christians ever since have construed it in terms not only of the Sermon on the Mount but also of the Cross on the Hill.

The word love always needs a dictionary, and for Christians the dictionary is Jesus Christ. He took this chameleon of a word and gave it a fast colour, so that ever since it has been lustred by his life and teaching, and dyed in the crimson of Calvary, and shot through with the sunlight of Easter morning.[1]

This is the *agape*, God's love in Christ reflected and responded to, which Paul celebrated in his best-known chapter. 'Love', he says, 'never faileth.' This we may take to mean that here is something which time can never render obsolete, a law of life as valid for us as for Paul's readers in Corinth, Colossae, Salonika or Rome. In our complex modern world it will never be easy to practise and apply. 'Love', Reinhold Niebuhr has said,[2] 'is always relevant but never a simple possibility.' Yet it remains the supreme principle of Christian action. 'When this is done, all is done.'

## NOTE ON THE NEW HERMENEUTICS

In Greek mythology Hermes was the messenger of the gods, as *hermeneus* is Greek for 'interpreter'. Traditionally therefore 'hermeneutics' has been the science of interpretation.

In our time, however, the old word has been repristinated by continental theologians like Bultmann, Bornkamm, Fuchs and Ebeling to describe the interpretation of biblical meanings in modern categories, especially those of existen-

[1] A. C. Craig, *The Sacramental Table*, 50.
[2] *Christian Faith and Social Action*, 12.

tialism, that philosophy, fathered by Kierkegaard and current since the Second World War in France and Germany, which radically concerns itself with individual and personal existence and holds that man must create values for himself by decision and action.

According to Bultmann,[1] the exegete's task is therefore to 'interpret the phenomena of past history in the light of man's understanding of his existence and so to make us aware of it as furnishing a basis for our present understanding. His duty is, by making the past present to bring home to us the truth, *Tua res agitur*: it concerns yourself.'

How then does this new hermeneutical method teach us to read the Gospels?

Just as long ago Jesus faced his hearers with his own presence and claims, which were indeed the claims of God, so today the Jesus of the Gospels confronts men with his words of grace and judgment, and summons them to decision (*Entscheidung*, a German word with which Bultmann peppers his pages) for life or death, i.e. for 'authentic' or 'inauthentic' existence.

Here in Britain where we are not steeped in existential concepts, much of this inevitably sounds strange. Yet, however alien the jargon of 'the new hermeneuts' may sound to us, none may deny their earnest concern to make the Bible speak to men in the language of our day.

How these 'existential hermeneutics' work out in practice may be seen in a book like J. W. Leitch's *The King Comes*[2] —an existential exposition of Mark 1-7; or in G. V. Jones's *Art and Truth of the Parables*[3] where Jesus' story of the Prodigal Son is made to speak to us of freedom and estrangement, longing and return, anguish and reconciliation.

---

[1] *Primitive Christianity* (London, 1960), 12.
[2] London, 1965.          [3] London, 1964.

IV

To be a Christian for Paul is to share in something which has happened, is happening, and will happen. It is the last of these tenses with which we are now concerned.

What Paul's Christian hope was we have seen. He believed not simply in an after-life for the individual but in a final 'wind-up' by God of human history, in the coming of Christ in glory, the resurrection, the last judgment, and a faithful rewarding by God of his saints in heaven. The question is, How far is Paul's doctrine of the Last Things tenable by Christians today?

There was a time when our eschatologically-minded forefathers found most of Paul's doctrine patient of an easy acceptance. These days are gone for ever. It is not merely that the old-style warnings of the flames of hell-fire have gone clean out of fashion, but we hear few sermons nowadays from Christian pulpits on that Day of reckoning so basic to Paul's thinking or on the high glories of heaven. Nowadays Paul's doctrines about the ultimate destiny of man and of the cosmos sound strange and even 'scandalous' to men taught to think in terms of evolution and 'the second law of thermo-dynamics' and it has been truthfully said that a Gallup poll on the question, 'What do you believe about a Second Advent?' held in an ordinary congregation, or even in a theological college, would be a shattering experiment.

On the other hand, our time has witnessed a revival of interest in the whole subject of New Testament eschatology, bringing with it much new light and understanding; and it is becoming clear that the time is ripe for a radical re-thinking, by our systematic theologians, of the whole Christian doctrine of the Last Things. For one thing, the history

of our times has shown that if the Church does not furnish
men with a credible religious hope, they will soon provide
themselves with secular substitutes for it, like Hitler's dream
of a *Reich* to last a thousand years or Marx's myth of a
classless society to supervene upon the final 'show-down'
between communism and capitalism. And, for a second
point, a Christianity shorn of an eschatological hope is a
Christianity which, in more senses than one, has no future
to it.

A Christian Hope then we must have; nor can we, in our
re-thinking of it, afford to neglect the insights of the
Church's first and greatest theologian. This does not mean
that we are therefore committed to a literal acceptance of all
Paul has to say about the Last Things. We must frankly
recognize that here Paul's statements, taking as they do the
form of myth and symbol, are neither inerrant prophecies
about the future nor pious guess-work. We appraise them
aright if we see in them rather 'transpositions into the key
of the hereafter of that sure knowledge of God which Paul
had found in his encounter with the living Christ'.[1] Our task
is to discover the truth embodied in Paul's 'transpositions'—
what is made sure to the heart by the witness of the Spirit—
and to translate it into contemporary terms.

Take first Paul's belief that the Resurrection of Jesus was
what we might call nowadays 'a breakthrough' of the
Eternal Order into this world of sin and death, an eschatological act of God, as new as the primal act of creation,
which inaugurated in miracle the New Age, involving not
only a new mode of life for Christ but also the promise of
life for all who were his, and assuring them that the Power
which took Christ out of the grave was available for them
not merely at the end of their earthly journey but here and
now.

[1] J. A. T. Robinson, *In the End—God* (London, 1950), 35.

If this is true, does it not mean that the Resurrection ought to bulk far more largely in our worship and our preaching than it does, that every Christian congregation ought to be 'a community of the Resurrection' and every Sunday in some sense an Easter festival? And ought not all of us who call Christ 'Lord' (a post-resurrection title) to be more vitally aware than we are that we are living in a world in which, for all its sin and sadness, Christ has left one gaping tomb in earth's wide graveyard and that his victory is like the breach in a North Sea dyke—an event of apparently small importance whose consequences are incalculable?

But Paul and his fellow Christians believed not only that Christ was risen but that he was now reigning. When they said, 'Jesus is Lord' they were not merely bestowing an honorific title on Jesus; they were affirming, with the full force of their minds and hearts, that he was now reigning over his People and the world.

*Christus regnat!* In the times of her great crises—as on the continent of Europe before and during the Last War— the Church has rediscovered the meaning of the ancient confession and found in it a battle-cry to inspire her in her fight with all the powers of evil. But unless Christianity is to degenerate into an arid antiquarianism, is not this note of a regnant Christ—a Christ who now rules and reigns over his People inspiring them, directing them, and does not sit simply in heaven like some retired and cloistered emperor —is not this a note which she must ever keep sounding?

Paul's eschatology, however, so far from being all 'realized', was steadily directed to the future, to the Day of Christ, the Parousia. In his earlier letters (as we saw) Paul expected its occurrence in his lifetime, though later he came to realize that he would not live long enough to see it. In fact, nineteen centuries have now gone by, and the Parousia has not yet taken place. What are Christians today to make of it?

Reflecting on the apparent delay of the Parousia, one early Christian writer wisely opined that time-measurements hardly applied to this event. 'Here is one point, my friends,' he said, 'which you must not lose sight of: with the Lord one day is like a thousand years and a thousand years like one day' (II Peter 3.8). Moreover, as C. H. Dodd has said,[1] certain sayings of Jesus about the Day of the Son of Man suggest that the early Christians were wrong in trying to fix its date at all because the Son of Man's coming is dateless; it lies outside our time-reckoning altogether. Does this mean that the doctrine of the Second Advent is of no importance to us?

This would be a rash and wrong conclusion. Belief in eschatology without belief in a real End, it has been said, is like belief in religion without belief in God. The fact is that we can neither take the doctrine literally nor dismiss it as unimportant. If we dismiss it as unimportant, we get a view of eternity which does not fulfil but annuls the process of history. If we take it literally—locate it in the time-series—we make the ultimate vindication of God *over* history (which is what the consummation of the Kingdom of God means) into an event *in* history, a mere point in it.[2]

What then should be its meaning for us today? Three things may be suggested. To begin with, it expresses the certitude of Christian faith that the Lord of history, who is the Father of Christ, will complete his saving work—that God must one day cry *Tetelestai* to the redemption which he took in hand when he sent his Son. Next, we should think of the Coming of Christ not as an event in history but

[1] *The Coming of Christ* (Cambridge, 1954), 7.
[2] R. Niebuhr, *The Nature and Destiny of Man* (London, 1943), II, 299.

as the point at which the race reaches its last frontier-post and encounters not nothingness but God in Christ: the point at which our time, i.e. human history and all in it well-pleasing to God, is taken up into his eternity. Finally, our clue to the nature of the Second Coming is the first one. God has already revealed himself in a Man by whom all may know what sort of Person it is with whom, at history's end, we have to do. We shall encounter the same Person whose holiness, truth and love we already know in Christ;[1] and if we have to appear before God's judgment-seat, we may believe, as Paul did (see Rom. 8.34), that the sign of the Cross will be over all.

What has Paul to teach us about the final state of the redeemed?

*First:* Immortal life is the gift of God in Christ. We are not immortal beings in our own right. Our hope of immortality is bound up with belonging to Christ, with 'Christ in us the hope of glory'. Only one life (he would tell us) has ever won the victory over death, and only one kind of life ever can win it—the life which was in Christ, which is in him, and which he shares with all whom faith makes one with him. What is important, then, is not the point of bodily death but the time when a man comes to be 'in Christ'.

Is not this the Christian truth of the matter still? Said Grenfell of Labrador: 'I have no more doubt that Christ lives in the world today than that I do myself. It is because he lives, and only so far as he lives in me, that I shall live also.'

*Second:* It is not as disembodied souls but as whole men that we shall live hereafter. Paul's was neither the crude

[1] Cf. Studdert Kennedy's lines:

> Then will he come, with meekness for his glory,
> God in a workman's jacket as before,
> Living again the eternal Gospel story
> Sweeping the shavings from his workshop floor.

Jewish belief in 'a resurrection of relics' nor the Greek belief in a ghostly disembodied existence hereafter. What he teaches in I Cor. 15 about the 'spiritual body' is an affirmation that the whole personality will be wonderfully renewed in the life to come, with all that is needed for its self-expression and power to communicate with others. And is not Paul's hope of a bestowal upon us by God, after the death of our present bodies, of new and glorious bodies that shall be the vehicles of a far higher life for the soul than any we are now able to enjoy, 'still the most reasonable hope for us today'?[1]

*Lastly:* The final state of the redeemed will be at once corporate and Christ-like.

The Hebrew, it has been said,[2] sees the life to come as life in society—a great feast: the Greek sees it as a somewhat lonely existence. So Paul, that 'Hebrew of the Hebrews', speaks of Christ as 'the first-born among many brethren', thinks of life hereafter as a family life—a great society of redeemed persons living for ever with the Lord. Not only so, but Paul declares that the Christian's destiny is to be 'conformed to the image of God's Son'. Thus he joins hands with St John: 'when he appears, we shall be like him' (I John 3.2). The apostolic hope is therefore completely, even Dominically, ethical. Men have painted many pictures of the heavenly state—unending sensual bliss, absorption into the All, Nirvana and the like. Paul and John hold fast what is Christianly essential. Salvation, full and final, is sharing the likeness of Christ, who is himself the image of God.

Such was Paul's Christian hope; and with that hope in view, does he not still summon us, as long ago he summoned the Corinthians, to labour unwearyingly in the Lord? By a

---

[1] J. Baillie, *And the Life Everlasting* (Oxford, 1934), 254.
[2] T. W. Manson, *On Paul and John* (London, 1963), 113f.

generation, all too this-worldly, too busied with 'getting and spending' and building its welfare states and paradises on earth, and too often forgetful that 'God has set eternity in man's heart', Paul's hope will be accounted as incredible otherworldliness and dismissed by many as 'pie in the sky when you die'. Those of us who hold it need not be unduly worried. Certainly Paul, if he were among us today, would not have been. He knew who it was in whom he had believed. For him the heavenly hope was no 'grand perhaps' but 'a solid weight of glory'; no 'opiate of the people' but a spiritual inheritance to challenge us to make our calling and election sure: 'a hope so great and so divine' as to beget in us immortal longings and to give human life a meaning and an end which the men of our day, groping about in darkness and despair, need more than anything else to make them feel that life is worth living, that Christ is God's master-clue to its meaning, and that 'the best is yet to be'.

# ABBREVIATIONS

AV     *Authorized Version of the Bible*

ET     *Expository Times*, Edinburgh

ICC     *International Critical Commentary*, T. & T. Clark, Edinburgh, 39 vols

JTS     *The Journal of Theological Studies*, Oxford

LXX     *The Septuagint*

NEB     *The New English Bible*

RSV     *The Revised Standard Version of the Bible*

TWNT     G. Kittel (ed.), *Theologisches Wörterbuch zum Neuen Testament*, Stuttgart, 1933ff.

# INDEXES

# INDEX OF AUTHORS

# INDEX OF SUBJECTS